Drs. 90

Spetsai

by

Andrew Thomas

Lycabettus Press

Published by
Lycabettus Press
39 Dimokritou
Athens 136
Greece
Telephone: 363-5567

Typeset by Fotron S.A.

Printed in Greece
by the Athens Publishing Center
24 Stratiotikou Syndesmou
Athens 136

CONTENTS

Acknowledgments

I would like to thank Byron Kesses and Adonis Kyrou for their help concerning the history and archaeology of Spetsai. Byron Kesses drew the plans of Kastelli and the Early Christian Basilica. He assisted Georgios A. Sotiriou during excavations on the island and his detailed information about Zogeria led me to discover the Byzantine gravestone referred to on page 45. I am grateful to the Greek Archaeological Service for the interest they have shown in the discovery and hope that more extensive excavations will take place in the future so that some of the gaps in my history section can be filled in. Georgios Stamatiou kindly provided me with information about the Anargyrios and Korgialenios School and its founder. I would also like to thank the owners of the island's *archontika,* who showed me round their homes and patiently answered my questions about their forebears for the purposes of this book.

Seti Sigalas drew the Spetsai waterfront panorama. The photographs on pages 16 and 17 were taken by Philippos Procopis and those on pages 15, 42, 53, 57, 62, 70, and 73 by Sheridan Ebbage. Peter von Hess's portrait of Bouboulina at the blockade of Nafplion appears by kind permission of the Director of the Wittelsbacher Ausgleichsfonds, Munich, who has asked me to mention that the vault in which King Otto and Queen Amalia of Greece are buried is in the Theatiner Church, Munich and is open to the public during the summer.

Spetsai, 1977   A.T.

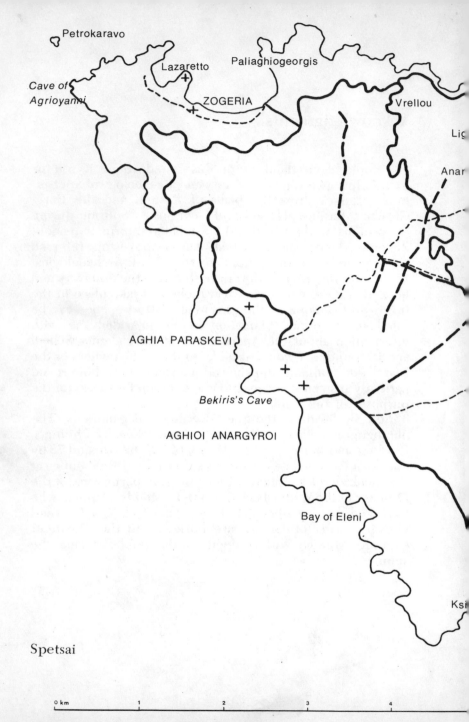

Petrokaravo

Cave of
Agrioyanni

Lazaretto

Paliaghiogeorgis

ZOGERIA

Vrellou

Li

Anar

AGHIA PARASKEVI

Bekiris's Cave

AGHIOI ANARGYROI

Bay of Eleni

Ksi

Spetsai

0 km   1   2   3   4

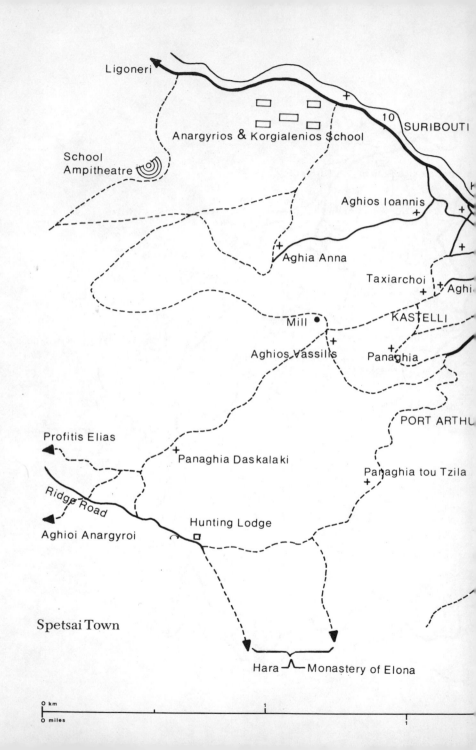

Ligoneri

SURIBOUTI

10

Anargyrios & Korgialenios School

School
Ampitheatre

Aghios Ioannis

Aghia Anna

Taxiarchoi

Aghi

Aghi

KASTELLI

Mill

Aghios Vassilis

Panaghia

PORT ARTHU

Profitis Elias

Panaghia Daskalaki

Panaghia tou Tzila

Ridge Road

Hunting Lodge

Aghioi Anargyroi

Spetsai Town

Hara Monastery of Elona

0 km   1

0 miles   1

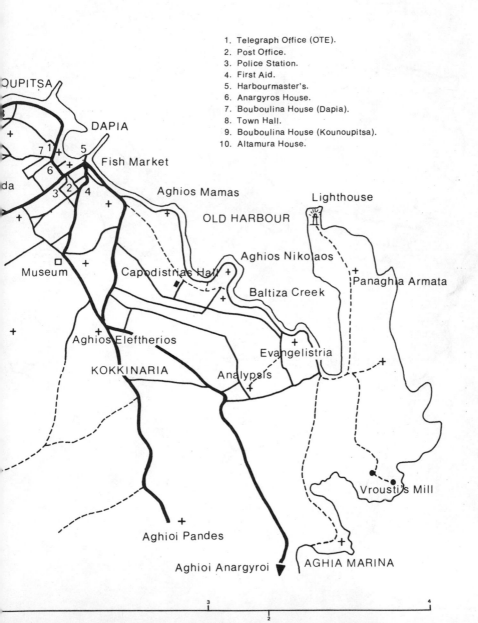

1. Telegraph Office (OTE).
2. Post Office.
3. Police Station.
4. First Aid.
5. Harbourmaster's.
6. Anargyros House.
7. Bouboulina House (Dapia).
8. Town Hall.
9. Bouboulina House (Kounoupitsa).
10. Altamura House.

OUPITSA

DAPIA

Fish Market

Aghios Mamas

OLD HARBOUR

Lighthouse

Aghios Nikolaos

Museum

Capodistrias Hall

Panaghia Armata

Baltiza Creek

Aghios Eleftherios

KOKKINARIA

Evangelistria

Analypsis

Vrousti's Mill

Aghioi Pandes

Aghioi Anargyroi

AGHIA MARINA

Introduction

The island of Spetsai lies at the entrance to the Argolic Gulf, 88 km. southwest of Piraeus, and 2 km. from the mainland of the Argolid. As Pityoussa, pine tree island, Spetsai is referred to by the 2nd century A.D. traveller Pausanias in his *Description of Greece.* According to Pliny the Elder, writing approximately 100 years earlier, the island had a good harbour, wells, was suitable for the cultivation of trees and vines, and had been occupied since ancient times.

Spetsai is an oval island, 7 km. long and 22 sq. km. in area. Its population is about 3,500, though this figure soars in the summer when there is a large influx of tourists. A number of houses are occupied only in the summer months, when their owners, many from Athens and Piraeus, are on vacation. The modern town of Spetsai has grown up along the northeast coast, around the island's two main harbours, *Paleo Limani* (Old Harbour) and Dapia.

The modern name *Spetsai* (in *katharévousa; Spétses* in the vernacular *demotiki)* has evolved from Pityoussa. The *s* prefix is probably derived from the Greek for *to* or *in.* Albanian settlers corrupted the original name to *Petsa,* which is how the island was known until the last century. The Venetians knew the island as *Spezie,* reminiscent of the port of La Spezia on Italy's west coast. It has also been suggested that the island's abundance of aromatic herbs prompted the Venetians to call it after *spezie,* the Italian for spices.

1

History

Excavations undertaken by Dimitrios Theoharis at Aghia Marina in 1970 and 1971 revealed seal stones and pottery indicating that the headland was the site of an Early Helladic settlement. The site extends from the shore near the present-day Church of Aghia Marina, inland of the bay to the north of the church. The now much eroded headland once provided greater shelter for vessels anchoring in this bay en route from the Cyclades to the Peloponnesos. In a well close to the shore were found fragments of dark-on-light painted pottery, incised ware, and cutting tools of obsidian, of the type found in the Cyclades. Other remains, including clay seals, spindle-whorls, and fragments of pithoi (large storage jars) confirm habitation here at the same time as there were settlements at Lerna, Tiryns, Argos, and Asine on the nearby Argolid.

Maritime commerce flourished during the Early Helladic civilization and Spetsai may have been a transit centre between the Greek islands and the mainland. The Early Helladic settlement on Spetsai seems to have been abandoned shortly before 2000 B.C., although no evidence of fire or violent destruction has been found. The discovery in 1975 of a ship, believed to be of this period, wrecked off the nearby island of Dokos, may throw more light on trade connections among the Aegean colonies before 2000 B.C.

Exploratory trenches northwest of the Church of Aghia Marina have revealed remains of the Late Helladic (Mycenean) period.

Marble remains found near the Church of the Analypsis may be, according to the Spetsiot archaeologist and historian Georgios Sotiriou, from a temple of Poseidon, but in the absence of excavations the existence of such a temple must remain in doubt. Other finds near the Church of the Analypsis near the Old Harbour indicate that the island was occupied during the late Roman period, and marble from Roman houses may have been reused as ornamentation in the island's two Early Christian basilicas. A Roman sarcophagus lid found in this area is now displayed in the museum. Sotiriou also found late Roman or Byzantine graves in a burial ground southwest of the church, in the district known as Kokkinaria. These graves are further evidence of the existence of a late Roman community on Spetsai.

In the 5th and 6th centuries A.D. the Old Harbour area was inhabited, though the extent of the settlement can only be estimated from the size of the two Early Christian basilicas excavated near Baltiza Creek and Vrousti's Mill.

Apart from a small number of fragments of Byzantine pottery no traces of occupation between the 9th and 15th centuries have been found on Spetsai, indicating that the island was not inhabited during this period. The island was probably abandoned because of Arab raids during the 9th century.

The earliest remains of the 16th century settlement known today as Kastelli are on a rocky plateau above the northwest side of present-day Spetsai town. It is impossible to say with any certainty from where the original settlers of Kastelli came. Sotiriou's theory is that Christian Albanians took refuge on Spetsai, possibly round the bays of Aghioi Anargyroi and Zogeria, after the fall of Mistras to the Ottoman Turks in 1460. Any theory, however, concerning the origins of the Albanian colonists who settled on Spetsai must be largely guesswork, for this is a poorly documented period of history for this part of Greece. Although Albanian was the predominant language spoken by these settlers, they also knew some Greek.

The earliest written source we have indicating that Spetsai was inhabited in this period dates to 1511, when Francesco Grassetto sailed close to the coast of the Argolid. This Italian traveller referred to Hydra and Spetsai (Specie) by name, but mentioned the other islands in the area only as "uninhabited outcrops of rock." The inhabitants may have been shepherd families which came across from Kranidion on the mainland in search of pastures for their goats. Local tradition holds that the first settlers came to the island in the 15th century and lived as shepherds in huts of pine,

3

depending for the necessities of life on their flocks and a crude form of barter (in olive oil, barley, dry legumes, cheese, etc.).

Many mercenaries fighting for the Venetians against the Ottoman Turks chose to settle on Spetsai rather than return to their native lands. They intermarried with the Albanians, and the Kastelli community extended farther down the hillside. In 1658 the Venetian M. Boschini noted that the island had few houses but enjoyed good fishing. It cannot have been until later, however, that fishing became the inhabitants' chief means of livelihood.

Kastelli lies 500 metres from the shore on a spur of the island's central ridge, protected on two sides by steep, narrow gulleys. The site commands extensive views of the Argolic Gulf to the west, the Argolid to the north, and the approaches to the Saronic Gulf to the east. It was chosen for safety against attacks by pirates and Muslim Albanians. The early inhabitants of Kastelli, from their vantage point a safe distance from the shore, had ample warning of approaching raiders, and could seek refuge in the pine woods which form a backcloth to the site. A fortress probably once dominated the crest of the hill on which today stand only a ruined windmill and the small Church of Aghios Vassilis. Houses must have occupied the area around the crest of the hill, but no traces of them are now visible.

The site was fortified by a strong wall enclosing an area approximately 620 by 300 metres reinforced at intervals by towers. The remains of this wall can be seen on the northeast, at the bridge of Aghios Georgios. Until the 18th century, the northern boundary of Kastelli was the rocky ledge below the Church of Aghia Triada. Around the Church of the Panaghia, the oldest in Kastelli, which served as a cathedral, were clustered shops, the school, and the public building where the elders of the community met.

The size of the town steadily increased during the 18th century, with the influx of colonists from Laconia, Kynouria, and the Argolid on the Peloponnesos, in particular after the surrender of Monemvasia and Nafplion to the Turks in 1715.

4

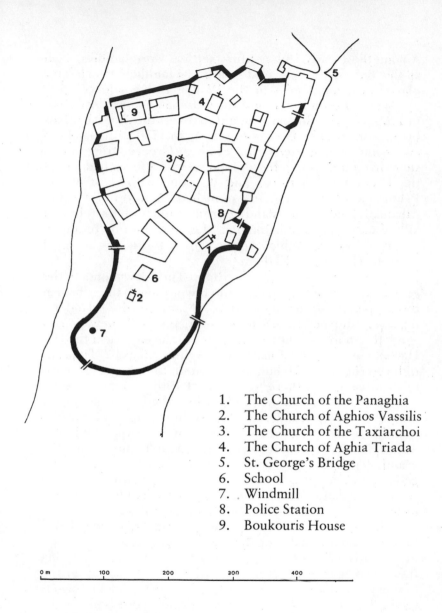

1. The Church of the Panaghia
2. The Church of Aghios Vassilis
3. The Church of the Taxiarchoi
4. The Church of Aghia Triada
5. St. George's Bridge
6. School
7. Windmill
8. Police Station
9. Boukouris House

0 m   100   200   300   400

Kastelli in the 18th century
Plan by Byron Kesses

5

Among these early 18th century settlers were families, such as the Botassis, Mexis, and Anargyros families, which later played prominent roles in the War of Independence.

War between Russia and the Ottoman Empire broke out in 1768, and the Russians sought to divert the Turkish forces by encouraging the Greeks to revolt. In 1770 a Russian fleet commanded by Alexei Orlov came to Greece, triggering a short-lived uprising in the Peloponnesos. Spetsai had joined the Greek-Russian forces and it, along with most of the Peloponnesos, was severely punished. A troop of Muslim Albanians raided the island, burning much of Kastelli and killing many of the inhabitants. Many escaped by hiding in Bekiris's Cave at Aghioi Anargyroi, or by fleeing in small boats to Hydra and Kythera.

Four years later, when the Russo-Turkish war ended, the Spetsiots set about rebuilding the town, though the Albanian threat persisted for some time. Many of the islanders, however, did not return to Kastelli, but built new houses along the shore beneath Kastelli and to the east, near the Old Harbour around the Monastery of Aghios Nikolaos. Time has reduced the pre-1770 houses of Kastelli to ruins, which have in turn been used there to construct 19th century houses.

Apart from the four churches described on pages 14-17, one of the last reminders that Kastelli was the heart of the island is a fine pebble mosaic to the west of the Church of Aghia Triada. Probably the oldest pebble mosaic on the island, depicting two-headed eagles, cypress trees, vases, and geometrical designs, it was laid in the courtyard of the 18th century Boukouris family home, no longer standing. It is now in the garden of a simple 19th century house.

The beginnings of the Spetsiot merchant fleet, which was to play a major role during the struggle for independence, are in the early 17th century, when the Spetsiots began building their own fishing boats of local pine. Shipbuilding on the island grew during the century and small craft of various types, but mainly the traditional caique, were built in the shipyards of the Old Harbour.

Larger trading vessels were built in the 18th century and

6

the island enjoyed an economic boom during the Napoleonic Wars, when Spetsiots frequently ran the British naval blockade of Mediterranean ports. As the profits of this daring commerce flowed into the island, so the shipowners began to build larger, better-armed brigs and schooners of 12 to 14 cannon. Despite the relative autonomy which Spetsai, in common with other islands of the Aegean, had been granted to neutralize the Russian influence in the area, the Turks were concerned about the growing strength of the island's fleet. Lascarina Bouboulina (see page 61) was summoned by the Porte to Constantinople to account for her shipbuilding activities. The Turks, however, were reluctant to curtail the maritime activities of the Greek islands, since increased commerce meant higher tax income for the Porte.

In the years preceding 1821, when the population of the island was approximately 8,000, the leading shipowning families had elected one of their own number mayor, or bey, the choice being ratified by the admiral of the Ottoman fleet, who was responsible to the Porte for the administration of the Aegean islands. Members of the local island council were also chosen from among the leading shipowning families. Two of these families, Mexis and Botassis, were always in contention for the highest position, and this rivalry continued in parliamentary elections well into the present century. The wealthy families favoured Mexis, while Botassis received the popular vote. Such was the ferocity of their disputes that local tradition maintains that the Ottomans despatched a supervisor to mediate their quarrels. The Ottoman official occupied the "Chancellery," a Venetian building destroyed by fire in the 19th century. In its place on the quay now stands the building housing the Harbourmaster's office.

To provide their fleet with more arms, Spetsiots used the pretext of needing better-equipped vessels to offset the continuing piracy of the corsairs based in North Africa. Spetsiot captains ventured farther and farther afield, to the Baltic Sea and even as far as America. Shipbuilding continued on Spetsai despite the recession which followed the end of the Napoleonic Wars. The Spetsiot historian Anastasios Orlandos maintains that most of the Spetsai ships ready for action at the outbreak of the War of Independence in March 1821 (54 fighting ships and a number of smaller craft) were built after 1810. Bouboulina's flagship, the Agamemnon, was completed just before the war began. The Hydriot Admiral Andreas Miaoulis was appointed commander-in-chief of the combined Greek naval forces, consisting mainly of the fleets of the three islands, Hydra, Spetsai, and Psara. Each fleet had its own commander and captains, often calling themselves admirals, who commanded the several fighting ships they had equipped.

The Philiki Etairia (Friendly Society — an underground freedom movement founded by Greeks in Odessa) played an

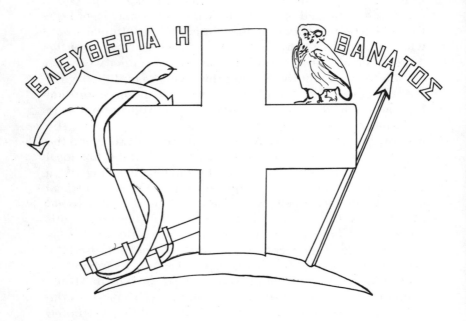

The Spetsai Flag

important part in organizing the fleet to support the struggle on the mainland. As early as 1818 many of the Spetsiot shipowners and captains had been initiated into the organization, and much of the wealth they had amassed from maritime trade went towards preparations for the rebellion.

As news of the revolt spread, Spetsiot ships hastened back to the island. The pulse of the Peloponnesos was also that of Spetsai, and as news of the acts of defiance reached the island, its leaders met to work out a plan. They agreed to approach the Hydriot leaders about a combined declaration of independence. By 2 April, however, Hydra had not responded, and appeals for naval support were coming from the Peloponnesos. That night, after an inconclusive meeting at the house of Georgios Panou, a prominent member of the Philiki Etairia, the younger leaders converged on the Chancellery, hauled down the Ottoman flag, and hoisted a cross in its place. They met with no resistance.

The following day, Palm Sunday, the people gathered at the Monastery of Aghios Nikolaos, the patron saint of the island and, after the service, the Spetsai flag was hoisted on the bell tower. The fleet, also flying the flag, lined up across the straits and fired cannons to salute the freedom of the Greeks. A procession marched to the Dapia, where the Ottoman official was ordered to leave.

At the instigation of Captain Ghikas Tsoupas, twenty-two Spetsiot ships sailed out to blockade the coastal forts of the Peloponnesos. Eight other Spetsiot ships, commanded by Bouboulina on the Agamemnon, sailed for Nafplion, which they blockaded until the Turkish garrison surrendered in December 1822. The fall of the fortresses at Monemvasia and Navarino in July and August 1821 was primarily due to the Spetsiot fleet cutting off relief supplies from the sea. The first Greek naval victory of the war was accomplished by Spetsiots, who captured two Ottoman ships at Milos. This success gave impetus to Hydra to join the revolt and, on 18 April 1821, a joint declaration was made by the three islands of Hydra, Spetsai, and Psara to coordinate their efforts against the Ottomans.

Spetsai remained one of the main bases of naval operations throughout the war. It had better anchorage than Hydra and its strategic position at the entrance to the Argolic Gulf was crucial. Control of the seas was vital to the Greek cause, and this the Greeks achieved despite the greater number of ships in the Ottoman fleet. The Greeks' skilled use of manned fireships contributed to their supremacy at sea. The Spetsiots excelled in this dangerous technique, which entailed approaching and in some cases securing the fireship to the enemy ship. The fireship, laden with combustible materials, was set on fire and then abandoned by its crew, all within close range of the enemy ship.

The Ottomans sought to relieve their garrison in Nafplion both by land and by sea. The land force was repulsed at Dervenakia north of Argos but, by the morning of 8 September 1822, eighty Ottoman warships had reached the nearby island of Trikeri. All the available cannon and ammunition on Spetsai were brought to the lighthouse headland. The Spetsiots, remembering the recent massacre at Chios, endeavoured to give the impression of having a well - armed force on the island. Popular tradition has it that red caps, worn in those times, were placed on the tall white spikes of the sea squill flowers growing on the headland. The Greek ships, scattered between Spetsai and the mainland shore, were ordered by Admiral Miaoulis to follow him to the entrance of the Argolic Gulf. The Spetsiot captains, however, seeing the Ottoman fleet advancing and fearing that the island would come under attack, ignored the order and engaged in battle. An indecisive exchange of fire continued throughout the day and the Ottoman fleet only withdrew at the sight of a Spetsiot fireship, commanded by Kosmas Barbatsis, which sailed out of the harbour late in the day. Apart from the loss of an Algerian ship the Ottoman fleet suffered no major damage, but it made no further attempt to break the blockade. By checking the enemy, the Greeks scored a great moral victory, and one of major strategic importance. The Ottoman fleet failed to relieve the beleaguered Nafplion, which fell just over two months later.

10

After the War of Independence, Spetsai did not maintain the importance it had enjoyed while the Peloponnesos was the centre of revolutionary activity. Part of this decline was the result of its war effort, which consumed much of its former wealth. The main cause, however, was a shift in the pattern of Aegean trade, as Syros and Piraeus became the commercial centres. The advent of steamships further reduced the importance of Spetsai's merchant fleet, though its shipyards continued to build fishing boats.

The efforts of the philanthropist Sotirios Anargyros (*see* page 67) early in the 20th century brought a degree of prosperity to the island. He promoted the construction of Daskalakis's cotton mill and himself laid the foundations for Spetsai's tourist industry by building the Posidonion Hotel. Older residents on the island look back with nostalgia to an earlier "Golden Age" of tourism between the World Wars when Spetsai boasted a casino and was renowned for its lavish receptions at the Posidonion Hotel for the British Navy, whose warships frequently dropped anchor in the straits between Spetsai and Kosta.

Nowadays, tourism is the main source of income. Nonetheless, many young Spetsiots continue the island tradition and join the merchant navy. The building of fishing boats continues at the Old Harbour, and fishermen send part of their catches to Athens. Agriculture has been on a minor scale since Anargyros acquired two-thirds of the island for planting pine trees. Although there are small flocks of sheep and goats, shepherds no longer bring their flocks across from the mainland to graze on the island. The Albanian language, spoken until this century, has fallen into disuse and lives on only in some of the local place names.

0 m   5   10   15

Plan of the Early Christian Basilica at Vrousti's Mill
Plan by Byron Kesses

Historical Sites

Early Christian Basilicas

The discovery by Sotiriou in 1937 of two Early Christian basilicas proved that the island was inhabited in or about the time of Justinian, in the second half of the 5th and first half of the 6th centuries A.D. Sotiriou excavated a small basilica measuring 17 by 12 metres near Baltiza Creek, partly covered by the 19th century Church of the Evangelistria. It comprised a narthex, nave, and two side aisles, separated by four columns. From its form, the remains of the stylobates, column bases, and other architectural fragments, the basilica has been dated to the second half of the 5th century. There is little to be seen on the site, since the basilica was covered on conclusion of the excavations. Some of the remains, along with photographs of the excavations, can be seen in the museum.

A somewhat larger basilica was discovered at the site known today as Vrousti's Mill. It lies between the Old Harbour and Aghia Marina, on a peninsula commanding magnificent views east to the islands of Hydra, Dokos, and Trikeri, and south to Spetsopoula and the southern Peloponnesos. Most of its materials have gone to the construction of two windmills, now ruined, standing at the east and west ends of the foundations.

The larger basilica is an apsidal building 27 metres long and 15.60 metres wide. It is divided internally by two colonnades, with a narthex 3.50 metres long covering the whole width. It has walls 0.60 metres thick. A court to the west paved with rough stone slabs corresponds to the aithrium of large basilicas. The two colonnades are each composed of five columns. The dating of the basilica by its architectural style to the 5th or early 6th century is confirmed by smaller finds, which include a Corinthian capital and forty Justinian coins.

The Churches of Kastelli

In common with most, excluding parish, churches in Greece, the four churches of Kastelli are locked. They are privately owned and maintained, but when approached for the key the owners or guardians willingly accompany the visitor to the church.

The Church of the Panaghia or Koimisis tis Theotokou (The Assumption of Our Lady)

To gain access to the Church of the Panaghia, visitors should ask at the shop near Lazaros's Taverna, above the bridge of Aghios Georgios, where they will be directed to the house where the key is kept. The oldest of the churches of Kastelli, the Panaghia was the cathedral of the early settlement. It is a 17th century church, built in the cruciform style with a dome. It was probably built during the same period as the Monastery of Aghios Nikolaos, of which it was a dependency. Set against a hillside of almond trees, which rises steeply to the Church of Aghios Vassilis, the Panaghia, with its split-level roof of red tile and small campanile with Venetian bells, provides a harmonious ensemble of architectural form. On its north wall, beneath the bell tower, are ceramic plates, said to have been placed there at the time of the church's restoration in the 1770's. In the forecourt outside the church is a small stone pillar. According to the Spetsiot historian Anargyros Hadzianargyrou, before the War of Independence repentant thieves returned stolen property to the pillar under threat of the priest's curse.

Inside, pillars divide the structure into a centre and two side aisles. The varying thickness of the columns, however, disturbs the symmetry. The cupolas and arches, as well as some of the walls, are richly decorated with frescoes, believed to be of the Cretan School of the 17th century. Some of the wall paintings have been covered with plaster, and the exposed frescoes bear witness not only to the fire damage caused by the Muslim Albanians after the Orlov Uprising, but also to that caused by the workmen's tools used to remove the

14

plaster. The wooden iconostasis is later than the church itself and the icons date from the 18th century. The replica of a boat, suspended in the centre of the church, is a votive offering of the kind commonly seen in island communities throughout Greece.

The Church of Aghios Vassilis (St. Basil)

On an imposing rocky elevation above the Church of the Panaghia is the small post-Byzantine Church of Aghios Vassilis (St. Basil). A single-aisled church, it once was the parish church of a sizeable community, although now it looks like a country chapel.

The Church of the Taxiarchoi (Archangels)

This church was founded in 1805 by a priest, Georgios Oikonomou. It is cross-shaped and surmounted by a dome.

Kastelli: the Church of the Panaghia

Inside is a gallery for the women in the congregation. An inscription in marble above the west portal describes how whoever should inherit the church would also benefit from the two vineyards of over five thousand vines at Ksilokeriza which went with it.

The Church of Aghia Triada (Holy Trinity)
    This is the largest of the Kastelli churches. According to the inscription on the marble lintel of the west door it was built in 1793 by the priest Emmanuel Papatheodoros. It is a

Kastelli: the Church of Aghia Triada

St. George and the dragon, from iconostasis in the Church of
Aghia Triada

three-aised basilica, with a dome and ten semi-domes. Its
chief feature is an elaborate wood-sculpted iconostasis. This,
the *epitafios* (the bier carried in the Good Friday procession),
the pulpit, the Bishop's Chair, and the lectern are the work of
the Papatheodoros family, three of whose members took
thirty-five years to complete the carving of the iconostasis.
This family still maintains the church and should be asked for
the key to open it. Information about the key can be obtained
from the shop on the left of the path going up to the church.

The Papatheodoros family have a wealth of stories about
the church. They relate, for example, how work on the
original church, intended to be dedicated to the
Evangelistria, was started three times over, but construction
was completed only after the founder's mother had a vision
that the church should be consecrated to the Holy Trinity.
Emmanuel Papatheodoros and his family are buried beneath
a marble disc in the centre aisle.

17

Museum

The museum (open daily 1000-1400 except Tuesday) is housed in an imposing mansion, once the home of Hadziyannis Mexis, one of the leading Spetsiot shipowners in the late 18th century. The mansion, which combines Moorish and Venetian influences, was built by Hadziyannis Mexis between 1795 and 1798. It is surrounded by high stone walls. Beside the entrance is a massive anchor, perhaps from an Ottoman ship, dredged from the sea near the lighthouse.

Dominating the stone courtyard is an impressive marble bust of Hadziyannis Mexis sculpted by Byron Kesses, who lives on the island. To the left of the entrance are the baker's ovens and a room where the dough was kneaded. To the right is an underground cistern and walled garden. Around the courtyard are busts of some of the naval commanders of the War of Independence such as Pavlos Hadzianargyrou, Anargyros Lembessis, Ioannis Kyriakou, Georgios Androutsos, Panaghiotis Botassis, and Lascarina Bouboulina.

The central doorway on the ground floor opens into a hall, containing a copy of a Venetian map, thought to be of Spetsai, dating from 1580; photographs of Kastelli; and a photograph of the citadel of Argos, at the foot of which Bouboulina's son, Yannis Giannouzas, was killed while defending the town in May 1821. The room on the right with a fireplace was used by the Mexis family to receive their guests. Portraits of the family and leaders of the Greek War of Independence are displayed on the walls.

The next room is dedicated to the family of Eleni Altamura, the Spetsiot artist of the last century (*see* page 65). It contains portraits of the artist; her father; and her son Yannis, himself a talented seascape painter. One of Yannis Altamura's works hangs above a photograph of the island taken in 1868. The size of the safe in the adjoining room gives some indication of the Mexis family wealth.

To the left of the entrance hall is the kitchen, containing a fine 18th century oven. A wood fire was lit beneath the structure, generating sufficient heat for the surface above to act as an extensive hot plate. Around the kitchen are examples of the copper, earthenware, and glass utensils once used on the island.

Next to the kitchen is another room with an open fire, the private living room of the Mexis family. In the winter months low divans covered with embroidered rugs and blankets were ranged round the fireplace. On the wall is a portrait of King George I of the Hellenes, at the age of eighteen. In the adjoining room is a cistern and a wooden staircase. This room led into Hadziyannis Mexis's office, now the museum office and closed to the public.

The first floor is reached by outside staircases. The steps on the left, by the mulberry tree, lead up to a room where a

The Hadziyannis Mexis House, now the museum

copy of the flag first flown by the Spetsiots during the War of Independence is on display. Spetsai's revolutionary flag was red and white and carried the emblems of the flag of the Philiki Etairia: a cross on a crescent, a javelin, an anchor, a snake, and an owl (sometimes a dove), symbolizing the fall of the Ottoman Empire and the ascent of Christianity, the certainty of victory on land and sea, overcoming the enemy (the snake) by the wisdom (or the purity) of the cause. It bore the motto: ΕΛΕΥΘΕΡΙΑ Η ΘΑΝΑΤΟΣ, freedom or death.

At the opposite end of the room is a casket containing the bones of Lascarina Bouboulina. She was buried at the cemetery of Aghia Anna, but her bones were later placed in the family vault at the Church of Aghios Ioannis. In 1928, to mark the centenary of the foundation of the modern state of Greece, the casket was placed in the Church of Aghios Nikolaos. It was moved to the museum in 1938, when the museum was established. The casket is flanked by pistols from the War of Independence. On the left is a painting of Bouboulina commanding a ship during the blockade of Nafplion. It is a copy of the painting by P. von Hess, painter to the 19th century Bavarian Court. Displayed on the walls are sabres, pistols, and other arms from the war. Many of the Greek revolutionary leaders are represented in the portraits hanging round the walls.

The next room is dedicated to the brothers Nikolaos and Athanasios Orlov. They were members of the Lazarou family, but took the name of the Russian admiral whom they actively supported during the Orlov Uprising of 1770. On display are a series of documents relating to the revolt, pictures of their ships, and cuttings taken from newspapers shortly after independence.

Of interest in the next room is the fireplace, at the back of which is the flue from the ground floor fire. In this room is a

Lascarina Bouboulina at the blockade of Nafplion
(by Peter von Hess)

collection of ceramics from the Far East, side by side with more familiar European china. It was originally a guest room. Beyond the wooden staircase, near which are two 19th century maps, is a room containing examples of Byzantine and post-Byzantine art. Outstanding amongst these is a silver icon of St. Nicholas, from Hadziyannis Mexis's ship. In this collection of ecclesiastical items are vestments from the churches of the island, and a finely carved wooden bier, with gold embroidery. There is a fine chandelier, while on the floor is a marble hatchment from the nearby Church of the Ypapandis (Candlemas) with the two-headed eagle, symbol of the Byzantine Empire.

The Archaeological Room contains finds from excavations made on the island:

1. Two marble Roman sarcophagus lids, and a Roman marble table found on the beach in front of the Anargyrios and Korgialenios School.
2. Fragments from the two Early Christian basilicas (5th and 6th centuries A.D.) excavated by Sotiriou at the Old Harbour and Vrousti's Mill.
3. Roman and Early Byzantine coins.
4. Various Christian antiquities, including clay lamps.
5. Earthenware pots and sherds found in the sea off Spetsopoula.

The heavier ancient marble remains from Analypsis and Kokkinaria are near the main entrance on the ground floor.

The last room on the first floor served as the women's quarters. One remarkable feature of the house was the existence of water closets, unusual in this period. The water closet in this room has been removed, but one may still be seen in the Flag Room.

Around the room are the painted wooden figureheads of some of the best known ships of the Revolution. Most of them are gods and ancient warriors, such as Poseidon, Lykourgos, and Epaminondas. The remainder of the room is a miniature folk museum, with examples of costumes, fabrics, and household utensils, which combine to build up an impression of life on Spetsai before, during, and after the War of Independence.

Returning to the wooden staircase, we climb to the second floor. Meetings of the island council presided over by Hadziyannis Mexis were held in this large room, with its carved wooden ceiling. The museum's library and archives, consisting of over one thousand documents concerning the leading Spetsiot families in the War of Independence, correspondence among many of the Greek leaders, and other papers concerning the local government of the island are kept here. The logbooks of the Spetsiot admiral Georgios Androutsos and his captains are of particular interest.

A door opens on to the terrace, from which there is a fine view over the town. With an uninterrupted view of the straits in both directions, ample warning was given of the approach of suspicious vessels. This terrace was the catchment area for the inner cistern on the ground floor. Behind the museum is the ruin of the house which belonged to another member of the Mexis family, Theodorakis Mexis. It once rivalled the Hadziyannis Mexis house in architectural splendour and its carved stone central staircase still stands.

Spetsai Today

Spetsai Town

The focal point of the island is the Dapia, which overlooks the modern harbour and quay. Throughout the year steamers from Piraeus moor at this jetty and the arrival of each boat arouses daily interest and curiosity. In the summer months the hydrofoil cuts travelling time to Zea Marina (Piraeus) to under two hours. A small car ferry operates a regular service between Spetsai and Kosta (on the mainland opposite) but a special permit from the police is required to bring a vehicle on the island Times of this and other boats are displayed on the notice boards near the quay.

Much of the activity in the harbour is from smaller boats; fishing caiques which moor at the quay in front of the Acropol Hotel and motor launches which anchor off the steps below the Harbourmaster's office. These motor boats ply between Spetsai and Kosta or Porto Heli, providing a convenient, if more expensive, alternative to the regular car ferry. From Easter onwards boats leave here for trips round the island, calling at Aghioi Anargyroi and Zogeria. Some also cross to

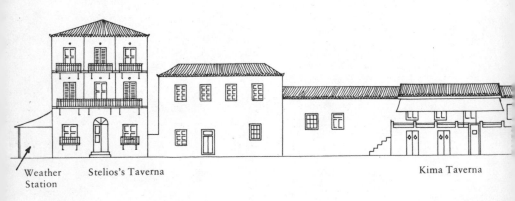

Weather
Station

Stelios's Taverna

Kima Taverna

sandy coves on the mainland. The largest launches operate day trips to Hydra, Nafplion, Leonidion, and Monemvasia.

Along the Dapia (a word of Turkish origin meaning a fortified place) cannons from the Greek War of Independence are still in place. Cafés now line the waterfront and tables are arranged outside on the pebble mosaics in the shade of pine trees. On some of the buildings round the Dapia are wall tiles painted by the ceramic artist Panos Valsamakis.

In the square behind the Dapia, overlooking a bust of Lascarina Bouboulina, is the imposing house which Sotirios Anargyros built in 1904. Egyptian sphinxes greet you at the foot of the white marble steps leading to the front door, outside which Anargyros's monogram is set into the marble. Entering the house, you are transported into a rococo setting of elaborately decorated walls and ornate moulded plaster ceilings. Art nouveau designs are on glass partitions and the ceramic fireplace. The Egyptian room has paintings of scarabs, birds, and lilies round the walls.

Close to Anargyros's house is a square in which a small children's playground has been made amidst the pines. On the right, a high wall overgrown with jasmine and bougainvillea surrounds a three storey L-shaped house. It is

Police Station 72-205
Harbourmaster 72-245
First Aid 72-472
Town Hall 72-225
Takis's Tourist Office 72-215

Soleil Hotel   Arcade   Fish Market

Newsagent

Bouboulina's house, in which her descendants still live. On the first floor is the large room where Bouboulina presided over meetings of the captains and crew of her fleet. Much of the original furniture has disappeared in the century-and-a-half since her untimely death, though the fine wooden ceiling and a safe from her flagship, the Agamemnon, have been preserved. Unfortunately, though a scheduled building of historic interest, the house is not open to the public.

Some of the island's *archontika* (homes of the leading families) have been occupied by members of the same family since their construction up to 200 years ago, and succeeding generations have striven to maintain their historic inheritance. Some, however, have come under new ownership or have fallen into disrepair as branches of families die out. The house of Ghikas Botassis, now hemmed in by a new cinema behind the Dapia, has altered little inside. The present owner points out with pride its hiding places and secret passage which concealed British soldiers during World War II. The family home of Ghikas's brother Anagnostis, built in 1802, is on the left of the street leading up to Lazaros's Taverna. The house's living room was a replica of the living quarters of Anagnostis Botassis's ship.

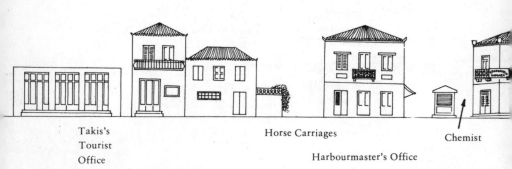

Takis's
Tourist
Office

Horse Carriages

Harbourmaster's Office

Chemist

Dapia to the Old Harbour and the Lighthouse

The sea road to the Old Harbour goes past the fish market and the town beach. Running parallel to it as far as the beach is a street above which are some fine 19th century houses. Just after a footbridge on the inner street is the island's weather station. Weather recordings are made by the Harbour Police, and enquiries about weather conditions may be made at the Harbourmaster's office by the quay. Overlooking the weather station is the Leonidas family home. Busts of two of its members, Georgios and his wife Chryssoula, greet visitors as they approach the steps leading up to a courtyard of pebble mosaics. Georgios is the son of Dimitrios Lambrou, who captained the warship Leonidas during the War of Independence; the family subsequently adopted the name Leonidas. Georgios's son built the house which was used as a casino during the late 1920's when gypsy minstrels provided musical entertainment. The long front room where the roulette tables once stood now contains a collection of family portraits and documents. The painted ceiling dates back to the middle of the last century.

On the first headland beyond the town beach is the small 19th century Church of Aghios Mamas. The road beyond this

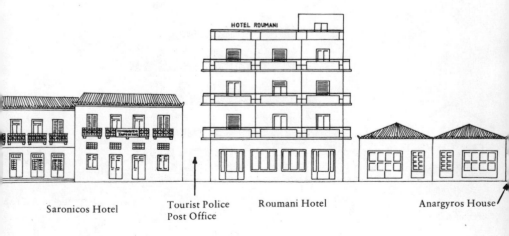

Saronicos Hotel   Tourist Police Post Office   Roumani Hotel   Anargyros House

27

point dates only from the beginning of this century and is occasionally damaged in stormy winter weather. Before it was constructed, the sea reached the foot of the rocky cliffs on which successful sea captains built their houses in the years succeeding the 1770 Orlov Uprising. The high walls served as a defence against sudden attack from the sea. A plaque on the first floor door of a house soon after the Church of Aghios Mamas reads "Institute of Modern Physics." The house belongs to Professor G.A. Zotos, a well-known Greek physicist, and he has equipped it with a laboratory.

Soon after passing the Zotos house you can see the Monastery of Aghios Nikolaos. Steps to the right of a small beach take you up to the oleander-lined path leading to the monastery. Beyond the next headland the road continues along what is called Baltiza Creek, past more fine houses. Soon after the monastery is the new church dedicated to the three Spetsai martyrs, Stamatis, Ioannis, and Nikolaos, young sailors who died for their faith on the island of Chios in 1822. Below, close to the steps in front of an attractive bar, sponge-fishing boats sometimes moor alongside other fishing and sailing craft.

Church of Aghios Antonios

National Bank of Greece

Star Hotel

OTE

Ionian and Popu

28

The harbour road takes you past Haralambos's Taverna, with its wooden platform built over the water. Dominating the Old Harbour is the grey stone house built early in the 19th century by the Botassis family. The walled courtyard is noted for its pebble mosaic of a mariner's compass. Below this, and separated from the harbour road by a lush garden of citrus trees, is the 19th century stone house with a whitewashed arcade belonging to the shipowning Goumas family. Farther southeast along the harbour road, beyond the picturesquely situated Old Bar, is the first of the four remaining shipyards for which Spetsai has long been famous. The timber, once from the pine woods of the island, now comes mostly from Samos. In the vicinity of the first shipyard are a number of small cafés. Fifty yards inland from the first shipyard is the small Church of the Evangelistria, partly covering the site of the smaller of the two Early Christian basilicas described on page 13.

The road rises over a small peninsula to another shipyard and the island's main slipway for the repair and launching of boats of up to seven foot draught. The larger caiques constructed on Spetsai are bound for the Libyan Sea and the fishing grounds off North Africa. The slope leads down to the

k

Acropol Hotel   Posidonion Hotel

inner harbour, which provides sheltered winter anchorage for yachts and caiques of all shapes and sizes. Here there is a marine filling station and access point for water. The road gives way to a path which skirts the shallow water at the head of the creek before joining the lighthouse headland. Another path across the field beyond the walled olive grove takes you to the peninsula on which two ruined windmills, known as Vrousti's Mill, mark the site of the larger of the two Early Christian basilicas described on page 13. From Vrousti's Mill the blue-washed Chapel of Aghios Dimitrios can be seen, crouching on the rocks below.

The path to the lighthouse goes past more shipyards and some barrel-vaulted buildings. The carpenter whose workshop is next to the barrel-vaulted buildings has the key to the Church of the Panaghia Armata on the lighthouse peninsula. To reach the church we continue along the path, past the French writer Michel Déon's house on the left.

The Church of the Panaghia Armata (Our Lady of the Armada) was built by the Koutsis family to commemorate the stopping of the Ottoman fleet in the Straits of Spetsai on 8 September 1822. In the church is a large oil painting purporting to depict the battle at its climax, close to the

(Goudis House)

30

headland. Beyond the church is the lighthouse from which, by looking westwards up the straits, you can see the mountains of the Peloponnesos rising above Argos in the distance.

Dapia to Ligoneri

The road from the Dapia northwest along the shore passes in front of the Posidonion Hotel, built by Sotirios Anargyros and opened in 1914. Between the two world wars it was frequented by leading European society and was the scene of sumptuous masked balls. Even today, the Anargyrios and Korgialenios School occasionally holds receptions for local and visiting dignitaries on the hotel's spacious terrace. The hotel incorporated the 19th century house built by Dimitrios Goudis. During quiet weather yachts moor at the jetty in front of the hotel while fishermen spread out their saffron coloured nets to dry on the promenade.

On the corner after the bridge is the Hadzipavlinas house, the first of a number of such mid-19th century houses. Their front doors face south, for these houses were built at the water's edge before the present coast road existed. The centrally placed outside stone staircase of these houses leads

Hatzipavlinas House

31

up either to an entrance hall on the upper floor or directly into a large central room. The central room extends the length of the house and opens out on to a balcony with wrought iron rails. The other rooms on the upper floor lead off the central room, while a trap door in the kitchen conceals a wooden staircase leading down to the ground floor. Several of these house have fine painted ceilings, the work of an Italian artist of the last century.

Beyond Hadzipavlinas Street is a large derelict building. Before World War II it was a cotton mill, built by Dimitrios Daskalakis in 1921. Its generator provided electricity for the island until about twenty years ago, and ice for the fish sent to Piraeus was produced here until the last decade. The building after the mill, with a terrace built on stone arches, is the Town Hall. It was the family home of Nikolaos Kyriakos, a Spetsiot captain during the War of Independence. It can also be approached from the inland street running parallel to the waterfront. Behind the house is an elaborate pebble mosaic of geometric designs, leading to an unusual semi-circular outside staircase. Portraits of Nikolaos Kyriakos and other distinguished Spetsiots hang on the walls round the central room.

Daskalakis Cotton Mill

The district near the shore west of the Dapia is known as Kounoupitsa. Kounoupitsa is the Albanian name for the Chaste Tree, a lilac flowering shrub in the Verbena family which grew in abundance here before the shift in population from Kastelli to the shore. On the corner where the inland street joins the waterfront at Kounoupitsa stands the house of another Spetsiot captain, Georgios Lembessis. The author of the short book *Spetsai,* Mina Tsallis, has lived here for many years. The inland street, between the Town Hall and the Lembessis house, goes past a tall stone house surrounded by a high stone wall. It is the house Bouboulina inherited from her first husband, Dimitrios Giannouzas, and where she was murdered in 1825. Visitors to the house will be shown the first floor window, overlooking the courtyard, at which she was shot. The designs of the pebble mosaics are among the finest on the island and include fish, animals, birds, and marine subjects.

The sea road at Kounoupitsa continues west towards the Anargyrios and Korgialenios School. The last of the sea front houses in Kounoupitsa, built in 1851 for the ship owner Michail Oikonomou, is the finest. It has ornate painted wrought iron window grilles. Although the rooms have been

Town Hall   Bouboulina House

stripped of their original furniture, the painted ceilings are a reminder of the house's former grandeur, when King George I of the Hellenes was a guest of the family. The kitchen contains an immense iron stove, taken from one of the ships of Oikonomou's merchant fleet of the last century.

The district west of the Oikonomou house is known as Suribouti, an Albanian name meaning fine sand. On the right, before the Spetses Hotel, is the house of the 19th century Greek artist, Eleni Altamura. Built by her seafaring father, Yannis Boukouris, it has an imposing doorway, flanked by cannons. Venetian glass lanterns stand on the tall entrance pillars. The high wall surrounding the house in which she became a recluse conjures up the name of Eleni's Italian husband, Altamura, but it must have been seen by the artist as protecting her from further misfortune in the outside world. Theodoros Dimitriadis (1896-1961), a descendant of Yannis Boukouris and author of *Kastelli*, lived here. He assembled an extensive collection of letters, documents, and portaits of the family, transforming the house into a private museum which, regrettably, is not on public view.

Two hundred metres west of the Spetses Hotel is the Anargyrios and Korgialenios School, founded by Sotirios Anargyros in 1927 and formerly under the patronage of the king. It is set in spacious and well-kept grounds, with a

Syntrivani   Lembessis House   Baker

stadium, tennis courts, open-air amphitheatre, and what must be the only Eton fives court on a Greek island. Beyond the school is the Kastelli Hotel. Then the road skirts round beneath a new holiday-flat complex before entering the pine woods of Ligoneri. Here there is a small chapel, standing near a spring which comes out of the rock, giving the locality its name, Ligoneri, or little water.

Dapia to Aghia Marina

The island bus to Aghioi Anargyroi, which leaves from the town beach, stops at Aghia Marina. It bears right at Stelios's kiosk and goes along the tree-lined street past the Church of Aghios Eleftherios, one of the largest on Spetsai and built in the 19th century. An alternative, more interesting route may be taken by people on foot or on bicycles by going from the Dapia along any of the lanes and passages to the Clock Tower Square. The clock tower was built in 1915 by Yannis Leonidas in an attempt to instil the habit of punctuality in Spetsiot children by getting them to school on time. Following the signs out of the square to the museum, we go eastwards past a large square house surmounted by an unusual watchtower. This house, as did the museum on the right after the crossroads, once belonged to the Mexis family.

Beyond the museum the street continues past the primary school, built in 1932, on the right, and the village secondary school, which occupies a large 19th century house on the north side of the road. The ochre coloured house beyond the nursery school was the home of Georgios Panou, a member of the Philiki Etairia who initiated a number of Spetsiots into the secret movement organizing the liberation. A marble plaque on the front wall of the house commemorates this and the meeting held here on the night of 2 April 1821, when the decision to revolt was discussed.

The tall three-story house beyond was the home of Captain Vassilis Lazarou-Orlov. From the garden door an unusual path lined with square stone pillars leads to the front door, above which is a plaque in honour of Lazarou-Orlov.

The courtyard and garden have an elaborate system, typical of that of the old houses, for channelling rain water into the cistern. The road crosses a bridge and continues past some shops to the crossroads by the Church of Aghios Eleftherios. The L-shaped house east of the church belonged to the Kalogeras family and served as a primary school until 1932.

Instead of turning right along the road to the Monastery of Aghioi Pandes, we proceed east to Analypsis Square, on the north side of which is the Church of the Analypsis (Ascension). Just before the square is an unusual doorway. The outside step has a pebble mosaic depicting an armed fighter, while the pediment above the door shows a gaff-rigged schooner, flanked by two anchors and the inscription "Arkadion, Crete, 24 May 1867." One explanation for this is that a Spetsiot ship, sailing off Crete at the time of the Turkish siege of the Monastery of Arkadion whose abbot chose to blow it up rather than surrender, brought back survivors who built the doorway as a mark of their gratitude.

After Analypsis Square, the road to Aghia Marina makes a sharp right turn to the south. It passes an open-air taverna, Aloni (threshing floor), and then the Twins Discotheque, named after twin-peaked Mount Didyma on the mainland opposite. From here the road drops gently to the Bay of Aghia Marina, where the lance-like cypresses on the hill above it guard the approaches to the Monastery of Aghioi Pandes.

By the road before the beach is George's, where there is live bouzouki music in the summer. Behind the beach is the Paradisos Taverna. A path from the north end of the beach climbs to the low cliff on which the Church of Aghia Marina stands. This area, excavated in 1970 and 1971, is the site of an Early Helladic settlement. A path from the church takes you past a shepherd's hut near a sandy cove, through the olive trees to the outskirts of the Old Harbour.

Doorway near Analypsis Square

The Monastery of Aghios Nikolaos

The Church of Aghios Nikolaos, the patron saint of fishermen and the sea, is known as the metropolis of the island. A number of paths lead to it past some of the finest houses on the island, from the gardens of which comes the scent of jasmine, roses, and honeysuckle on summer evenings. The stepped pebble mosaic path from the bridge behind the town beach passes the old village school, now fallen into disrepair. Built in 1830, it was one of the first primary schools to be built by the independent Greeks and it was regarded as recognition of the Spetsiots' efforts in the War of Independence. After 1932 when classes were transferred to the new school, the building was renamed the Capodistrias Hall and was used for public meetings and to house a small library. In front of the now derelict building is a

The Monastery of Aghios Nikolaos

bust of Georgios Sotiriou (1880-1965), the Spetsiot archaeologist and historian, who for forty years was director of the Byzantine Museum in Athens.

The path, lined with pink and white oleander, opens into a square in front of the monastery. In this square, made up of pebble mosaics, including one of Bouboulina, parades and processions begin on important days in the religious and civic calendar. Opposite the monastery is a war memorial, a bronze cast of the Spetsai flag. Dominating the square is the fine white marble campanile, of the type often seen in the Ionian and the Cyclades islands. On this campanile the Spetsai flag was hoisted to mark the beginning of the struggle for independence against the Turks, on 3 April 1821. Below the square is a small olive grove belonging to the monastery.

Little is known with any certainty about the early years of the monastery. It was built early in the 17th century and the Church of the Panaghia in Kastelli was a dependency of it. At that time it stood alone above Baltiza Creek, and it was not until after the destruction of Kastelli that the monastery became the heart of the Old Harbour community, when houses sprang up on the ridge over the creek and along the shore. The oldest existing wall is on the east side, and original defensive loopholes are still visible near the top. Monastic life continued until the War of Independence, when the cells around the courtyard were occupied by nuns. In recent years they have housed archives and for a time they functioned as classrooms for the secondary school. The library from the Capodistrias Hall, now kept here, can be visited on application to the Town Hall.

An inscription over the door of the porch supporting the campanile records that extensive repairs on the monastery were carried out and the campanile was built in 1805. At about this time the status of the church was raised to metropolitan, reflecting the shift in population to this side of the island. The repairs and the construction of the campanile were financed by contributions from the three constituent groups of the island hierarchy: the gentry, the shipowners, and the property owners. In the courtyard and arcades around the church civic meetings were held in the early 19th century.

During the War of Independence the body of Paul Bonaparte, a son of Lucien, the brother of Napoleon, was kept in a barrel of rum stored in one of the monastic cells. Paul Bonaparte, a Philhellene who had come to Greece to participate in the liberation struggle, was accidentally killed in 1827 when his pistol exploded while on board Admiral Cochrane's flagship, which was sailing close to the island. (Early in 1827 the Greek government had invited Cochrane to take command of the Greek navy.) Paul Bonaparte's body was kept in the monastery five years until it was taken on a French warship to Sphakteria, near Navarino, to be buried.

The cells on the ground floor have remained virtually unchanged. Stone staircases from the courtyard lead to the rooms on the upper floor. Sunday school classes are held here and one room is kept as the bishop's room, Spetsai being in the Diocese of Hydra. From the raised walk above the arcades you can see colourful enamelled plates of Italian origin set into the north wall below the dome. There are good views to the east of the harbour and lighthouse.

The church is built in the form of a cross, surmounted by a dome supported by four columns. Formerly, the walls were covered with frescoes like those in the Church of the Panaghia in Kastelli. The gilt and painted wooden iconostasis predates the 1805 repairs. On it there is a silver icon of St. Nicholas, dated 1798, but the other icons in the church are 19th and 20th century.

The Monastery of Aghioi Pandes (All Saints)

The Monastery of Aghioi Pandes occupies the hill above Aghia Marina at the top of an avenue of cypress trees. The cemetery in which Sotirios Anargyros and other famous Spetsiots are buried is on the right. A wall skirts the grounds belonging to the monastery in which the nuns maintain a small farm (monastery is a generic term in Greek, used whether the institution is inhabited by monks or nuns).

The oldest part of the monastery is the church itself, built in 1804. It is of simple design, with a campanile. Inside, however, it is richly decorated with a wooden iconostasis and a host of icons, one at least reputed to be of Russian origin. The rooms on the right of the church are reception rooms for visitors, who can enjoy the view of the islands from the wooden benches in the shade of the pine tree. Near the church are the tombs of two leading Spetsiot bishops, Nikiforos Kalogeras (1835-1896) and Andreas Triantafillou (1883-1938). The pyramid north of the church is the tomb of the local philanthropist Dimitrios Goudis (1824-91), who financed the construction of the Dapia harbour walls. The tomb contains a bust of him sculpted by Dimitrios Philippotis (1839-1919).

The monastery was founded in 1833 by Sophronia Ghinis, wife of the Spetsiot captain Vassilis Ghinis. As had her formidable contemporary, Bouboulina, she had sailed with her husband and participated in naval battles during the War of Independence. When her husband was appointed by the new King of Greece, Otto, as commissioner of the Cyclades in 1833, she rebuilt the Church of Aghioi Pandes and added twenty cells so it could function as a monastery, of which she became the first Mother Superior.

The Monastery of Aghia Anna
The Monastery of Aghia Anna stands on a hill west of Kastelli. It is best approached from the Church of Aghios Ioannis in Kounoupitsa, along a road through olive and almond trees. Before 1821 Spetsiots buried their dead in the cemetery near the monastery, which then extended over a wider area than it does now.

The modern Church of Aghia Anna is built on the site of an older church. It is in a peaceful setting of vines, olive, and fruit trees, overlooking the grounds of the Anargyrios and Korgialenios School, an ideal spot for the local artist and sculptor, Byron Kesses, to construct the small Byzantine basilica and monastery he designed. The rooms provided for the nuns lie to the north of the church. The central room, built in traditional island style, contains furniture collected from the family homes of the town.

41

The new church was built between 1966 and 1969. The altar table of the original church was retained, while the iconostasis, despite the use of modern materials, is reminiscent of Byzantine marble iconostases of the 11th century. There are some fine 18th century candlesticks, and the icons are the work of monks who visited the island in the 18th and 19th centuries.

Kounoupitsa: pebble mosaic in the courtyard of the Bouboulina House

Excursions on the Island

Aghioi Anargyroi

The only settlement other than the town of Spetsai on the island has grown up on the southern shore, around the Bay of Aghioi Anargyroi. Until recently the village consisted only of two churches, a farmhouse, and isolated shepherd dwellings, but recently some summer homes have been built, mainly on the west side of the bay. Aghioi Anargyroi, nevertheless, remains calm and uncrowded in a great natural amphitheatre formed by the terraced slopes rising up to the pine woods surrounding the bay on three sides.

The road leading down to the bay from the coast road ends abruptly beneath a tall pine tree, part of a green fringe of vegetation bordering the sand and pebble beach. Boats from the Dapia moor off the jetty opposite this point. Beside the road is a 19th century church dedicated to the saints Cosmas and Damian, known as *anargyroi,* the penniless. Cosmas and Damian were 3rd century physicians in Asia Minor who tended the sick without payment, hence their name. It is said that the bay owes its name to refugees from Laconia, the mountainous province of the Peloponnesos, visible to the southwest. They are thought to have settled here in the early years of the Ottoman Empire, bringing with them icons of the Penniless Saints. Beside the church is an open-air taverna, open from Easter till October. On the hill above the taverna is another church dedicated to the saints Cosmas and Damian. This second church was built this century on the site of a much earlier church, of which the foundations are still visible in front of the south door.

A cliff path leads from the west end of the beach past a ruined lime kiln to Bekiris's Cave. Before the last century the cave provided a safe hiding place from pirates raiding the island and it was here that Spetsiots sought refuge during the devastating raid by the Muslim Albanians after the Orlov Uprising in 1770. Once it could only be entered from the sea, but now steps lead down through the narrow fissure in the rock providing access from the cliff. Narrow steps and a causeway lead into the depths of the cave, where the only light comes through the sea entrance. The floor of the cave is sandy and stalactites hang from the low roof. In the centre fresh water drips from a stalactite into a natural bowl, hollowed out from a massive stalagmite formation which extends into the sea.

The cliff path continues past Bekiris's Cave to a headland, from which can be seen the Moorish arches of Villa Yasemia, standing high on the promontory before Aghia Paraskevi (*see* Walk Four p.50).

Aghioi Anargyroi

Zogeria

The Bay of Zogeria is on the northwest side of the island. Although accessible along the rough track branching off the road round the island, it is best reached by boat. Throughout the summer boats regularly leave the Dapia for the small Bay of Lazaretto, separated from the Bay of Zogeria by a narrow headland.

It is believed that there was a settlement around the bay in Early Christian times, for sherds from this period have been found here. Preliminary excavations on the headland beyond Lazaretto suggest that it was the site of a Roman or Early Christian watchtower, the base of which can still be seen. At Paliaghiogeorgis, the headland on the east side of the bay, there once stood a Church of Aghios Georgios, the remains of which are mostly concealed by dense undergrowth. Near the ruins the author discovered a marble gravestone with a Byzantine inscription dating to the 6th century, now in the museum. East of the site of the old church is a ruined lime kiln and traces of early habitation are visible on the wooded promontory above Paliaghiogeorgis.

Close to the jetty in the Bay of Zogeria is the Church of the Analypsis, built in 1834. On the headland west of Zogeria stands the 19th century Church of Aghios Georgios. Tall agaves (aloes) grow beside the path across the headland. The name Lazaretto comes from the Italian for a quarantine hospital. The Spetsiots built a hospital here in the 18th century for Greek sailors to recuperate from diseases they contracted during travels in their merchant ships. Little remains of the once extensive buildings except their crumbling walls and the cobblestones of their courtyards, now a favourite haunt of the Scops owl. Beside the ruins is the wooden hulk of an abandoned sailing boat.

Upturned cannons, now used as bollards, line the shore, rusty relics of the War of Independence. During the summer months when Loula's Taverna is open you may find Kyria Loula sitting outside her kitchen. She has a store of recollections, including the time she gave Melina Mercouri, a frequent visitor to the island, an informal shower from a jug.

45

Zogeria: the Church of the Analypsis

Loula's husband, Barbayannis, is one of the few people who can show you the overgrown path through the pine trees and heather to the Agrioyannis Cave. The cave is just north of the western tip of the island, on which a small shrine has been erected. Only cave enthusiasts should attempt the difficult descent into this unlit cave.

Walks

Visitors to Spetsai are recommended to explore the island on foot, for only on foot can the stillness and fragrance of the extensive pine woods be fully appreciated and the bird, animal, and plant life be closely observed.

Walk One: To Hara and the Monastery of Elona

Follow the road from the Dapia to the Monastery of

Aghioi Pandes, passing the Church of Aghios Eleftherios in the part of town called Kokkinaria. At the bottom of the tree-lined slope leading to the monastery, leave the road and branch right on a path to the south. This path takes you up the hillside with good views of Aghia Marina. As the path climbs higher Spetsopoula comes into view and, below, between Aghia Marina and Kouzounos, the extensive olive grove which Stavros Niarchos has on Spetsai can be seen. Cereals are cultivated on the narrow terraces on either side of the path. Behind, the Monastery of Aghioi Pandes appears in the midst of tall cypresses.

The path continues to a ridge from which Spetsopoula and the northeast corner of Spetsai can be seen clearly. If the weather is clear the mountains of the southern Peloponnesos can be seen in the opposite direction, rising above the sea to the southwest. Higher still, on the island's central ridge among the pine trees, the path reaches the small chapel dedicated to the Three Spetsai Martyrs, privately owned by the Botassis family. From the chapel, overlooking the sprawl of whitewashed, red-tiled houses in Spetsai town, you can see the mountains of the Argolid rising to the north beyond the straits separating Spetsai from the mainland. On the mainland shore, where a narrow headland juts east into the sea, stands the small white Church of Aghios Emilianos.

Near the Botassis' chapel are three graves, each covered with a pebble mosaic in a simple floral design. Here, high above the town they shunned, are buried Maria Botassis, the poet; her sister, Irini; and Irini's Swiss officer husband, Hermann Weissenberger. Superstitious villagers tell mysterious tales about the strange life and death of this eccentric family. A path covered in pine needles leads to the house where they lived in the first half of this century. Above the gate, in large wrought iron letters, is the word *XARA*, Hara (Joy).

Maria Botassis, born on Spetsai in 1880, was the first of the sisters to return after studies and a cosmopolitan life in Switzerland. Although not a prolific writer, several of her poems were published in Greece between her return in about

1930 and her death in 1961. The religious and romantic essence of her poetry is clear even from the titles: "Hermit of the Rock," "What I dream," and "Prayer to the Woods." Much of her imagery is that of the solitude of the woods around her. For one whose poems reveal such a love of nature, the simple floral mosaic on her grave is a fitting epitaph.

Southwest of Hara, on a spur of the central ridge, is the Monastery of Elona. The name Elona means Zoodochos Pighis (Well of Life i.e. the Virgin Mary) in Albanian. It was founded at the end of the 19th century, but its monastic life lasted only into the first years of this century. The grave of its founder, Akakios Koutsis, is just outside the church door. Now the cells around the courtyard stand empty, and there is activity here only on the Feast of Zoodochos Pighis.

To return directly to town, retrace your steps to Hara. Continuing north, leaving Hara on your right, take the mule track beside the wall skirting the Botassis property leading down to a spring and eventually the road to the Monastery of Aghioi Pandes on the outskirts of town.

Walk Two: to the Churches of Profitis Elias and Panaghia Daskalaki

Leave the town by the road up the hill past the Police Station and, higher up, Lazaros's Taverna. Kastelli is to the west as you follow the track going past the Church of Aghios Adrianos and its cemetery. From the church there is a good view of the old and new houses of Kastelli, with the domed churches of Taxiarchoi and Aghia Triada prominent on the ridge.

Having left the town, the path rises steadily to the locality known as Port Arthur, passing first an old walled house on the left and later the small Chapel of the Panaghia tou Tzila and a circular threshing floor on the right. From here it is only a short climb to the hunting lodge (Συνάντησις Κυνηγῶν) on the central ridge. The ridge road goes west from the hunting lodge past some ruined houses. On the left is a series of narrow stone terraces which once held rows of beehives, rising to an overgrown ruined house. This once belonged to Dimitrios Leonidas, who owned the island casino. Continuing along the ridge, you pass the turning to Aghioi Anargyroi on your left. Shortly thereafter, on the highest point of the island (252 metres), stands the Church of Profitis Elias (Elijah). To the southwest the peaks of the Parnon range of the southern Peloponnesos rise like a steep wall behind Leonidion. To the north the town of Kranidion nestles in the low hills opposite Spetsai and the mountain of Didyma rises above it on the horizon.

Return along the ridge road to the path marked to Aghioi Anargyroi, then turn left along a path to the north side of the ridge and the Church of the Panaghia Daskalaki. This church was the private chapel of Dimitrios Daskalakis (1860-1939), whose grave lies by the north wall. Daskalakis was a Cretan refugee who became a mill owner in Piraeus. He was a close friend of Sotirios Anargyros, who encouraged him to start a cotton mill, which opened in 1921, on Spetsai. The mill now lies derelict on the waterfront west of the Posidonion Hotel. Daskalakis spent summers up here among the pine trees, in a house overlooking his mill. From the chapel you can see to the northwest the rocky islets of the Gulf of Tolon, towards Nafplion: Psili, Plateia, and Rombi.

A path which winds through the pine trees leads to the ruined windmill and the Church of Aghios Vassilis, above Kastelli. A maze of paths between old stone walls takes you down into the centre of the town.

Walk Three: To the Bay of Aghioi Anargyroi
Make for the central ridge of the island, either by taking the track past Lazaros's Taverna or the path to the Church of Aghios Vassilis in Kastelli. Between the hunting lodge and Profitis Elias is the signpost to the path leading down to the southern shore of the island. On all sides the pine trees sweep down to the sea in a continuous wave. The gradient of the path is made more gentle by loops, some of which can be cut off by the surefooted.

Just above the Bay of Aghioi Anargyroi, where the pine

and olive trees merge, a small number of holiday homes have been built. The path joins the road round the island before an old farm on the corner where the road branches down to the beach.

Small boats call here, and the island bus halts at the taverna during the summer, but services are irregular and walkers hoping to find transport back to town should make sure that some will be available before they set out. Those who are determined to return on foot may return as they came or may climb back up to the central ridge along the fire-break. A way has been cleared through the trees from the farm at Aghioi Anargyroi to the ridge.

The fire-break continues on the north side of the island, and to rejoin it turn east for a short way along the ridge road. The fire-break will lead you down the spur above the Anargyrios and Korgialenios School, but about halfway down a path leads off from the fire-break to the east. This path forks after passing a narrow path meandering towards Kastelli. The fork to the left goes to the school's observatory and open-air amphitheatre, and the fork to the right goes to the new Monastery of Aghia Anna. From Aghia Anna the path goes by the cemetery into the part of Spetsai known as Kounoupitsa.

Walk Four: To Aghia Paraskevi and Villa Yasemia, "The Magus's house"

To reach the path which descends to Aghia Paraskevi on the south coast of the island, climb to the central ridge by one of the two routes suggested previously. Continue northwest along the ridge road well beyond Profitis Elias and the first fire-break until the Bay of Aghioi Anargyroi is some way behind you. Take the path leading off the ridge road along the second fire-break. The path along the second fire-break goes to a rocky outcrop overlooking the islet of Petrokaravo, off the island's northwest headland. At the foot of this outcrop is the path to Aghia Paraskevi. This point can also be reached by continuing on the ridge road as it weaves down through the trees and turning left on to a second path turning off the ridge road to the south. Though at times narrow, this second path is a gentler approach to the Aghia Paraskevi turning.

50

From the foot of the rocky outcrop a well-constructed path, at times banked up by stone walls, leads down the spur towards Aghia Paraskevi. To the east a broad cultivated valley drops down to Aghioi Anargyroi, while to the west the pine trees reach down to the shore itself at Aghia Paraskevi. The path ends abruptly, shorn off by the new coast road. It brings you down opposite an imposing gateway, the entrance to Villa Yasemia (Jasmine). This is the so-called "House of the Magus,"which readers of John Fowles's *The Magus* know as "Bourani." The house stands high on the promontory between the two bays and is best seen from the sea. It is said by the owner to have been built on the site of a ruined monastery, but now the gleaming white Moorish arches and Romanesque windows have become a landmark for hunters of literary monuments. The present owner is a descendant of one of the Botassis brothers who distinguished themselves during the War of Independence, and the house contains many relics of that period. It is private property and not open to the public.

It is a short walk from Villa Yasemia down to the cove of Aghia Paraskevi. The Church of Aghia Paraskevi is among the pine trees which stretch down to the half-sand, half-shingle beach. The church's bell hangs from a pine tree nearby. The church was built early in the 19th century, and icons of that period hang to the right of the south door and above a door leading into an anteroom.

If the walker wishes to return to town by a different route, he may walk back along the road past Villa Yasemia to Aghioi Anargyroi, where he can either take the path suggested in Walk Three or catch a boat or the bus back to the Dapia.

Since the island is interlaced with paths and mule tracks, the possibilities for walks are by no means exhausted with these four suggested routes. Less enterprising walkers may prefer to stick to the coast road, though the full distance round the island is 25 kilometres.

Eating and Drinking

Visitors to Greece are often bewildered by the distinctions among what are loosely translated as the coffee shop, the restaurant, and the cake or sweet shop. Greek coffee is served at a *kafeneion,* as are ouzo and Greek brandy, but little else. A glance through the window will suffice to bring home to the visitor that the *kafeneion* is a man's preserve, where the men assemble for a coffee, intent on their cards or backgammon, though nowadays it is not uncommon to see women sitting at the tables outside.

In Greece, if you have time on your hands, you can have a meal in three stages. Starting at the *kafeneion,* you can order a glass of ouzo which will be served with a small plate of hors d'oeuvre, a *mezé.* A taverna will provide you with your main courses. Since tavernas rarely serve more than fresh fruit to follow the meal, you can turn for a dessert to a *zacharoplasteion,* which also offers a wide range of drinks.

There is no shortage of places to eat and drink on Spetsai. The main street out of the Dapia up the hill past the Police Station takes you to Lazaros's Taverna, open in the evenings, where you can be sure of finding a lively atmosphere. Most of the island's tavernas now have jukeboxes and spontaneous dancing is a frequent occurrence. At the Old Harbour, fried squid is a speciality at Haralambos's Taverna, popular with the sailing community, while inland from Analypsis Square at the Klimataria (grape arbour) you can eat in quiet, unspoiled surroundings. The Orange Doors Taverna is convenient for the town beach, as is Stelios's Taverna nearby. Between the town beach and the fish market is Klimis's *zacharoplasteion,* which specializes in *loukoumades,* small fried doughnuts covered with honey and cinnamon. Their *amygdalota* resemble almond Turkish delight.

From the terrace of the Kima (wave) taverna by the sea road near the fish market you can watch the boats crossing from the mainland. Paraskevas's Grill in the Clock Tower Square is noted for its chicken and *kokoretsi,* grilled sweetbreads of lamb, popular at Easter. At the *kafeneion* by the fish market you will be served *marithes* (whitebait), squid, or octopus as a *mezé*. Having been tenderized on a rock, the squid and octopus can be seen hanging up to dry.

There is one taverna on the Dapia. At Yiannis's you may sit outside on a fine pebble mosaic and survey the promenaders while sampling some of the Greek dishes which have become well-known outside Greece: *moussaka;* stuffed tomatoes; courgettes; and *papoutsaki,* "a little shoe" of stuffed aubergines with cheese sauce. The *zacharoplasteia* round the Dapia sell the Spetsai speciality, *amygdalota,* small cone-shaped almond cakes covered in icing sugar and flavoured with rose-water. Another almond cake, known as *ergolavos,* similar to a macaroon, is a speciality of the *zacharoplasteion* beside the Church of Aghios Antonis.

The Old Harbour

There are three tavernas between Spetsai town and the Anargyrios and Korgialenios School. At the Kypros (Cyprus) Taverna you can eat at tables on a wooden platform at the water's edge. Further northwest along the sea-road are two tavernas noted for fresh fish, Patralis's and Zammas's, the latter also known as *To Nero tis Agapis* (The Water of Love), after a nearby well on the estate which once belonged to Bouboulina.

In addition to the tavernas serving traditional Greek food, there are restaurants with more ambitious menus, offering both Greek and international dishes. The Trehandiri (small caique) restaurant overlooking the Old Harbour near the Monastery of Aghios Nikolaos is noted for its seafood. The Syntrivani (fountain) near the Town Hall and La Lampara (named after the lamp on the bow of a fishing boat), an Italian restaurant in front of the Anargyrios and Korgialenios School, provide alternatives to solely Greek fare. Spetsai, however, is the home of one of the most popular fish dishes in Greece, *Psari Spetsiotiko* (Fish à la Spetsiota), and nowhere is it better prepared than at Lyrakis's Restaurant, the Mandalena, above the arcade near the fish market. Sea bream is the fish generally used for this speciality, which is served with a rich, highly seasoned sauce.

Where To Stay

Hotels

The Posidonion Hotel is prominent on the waterfront to the west of Dapia harbour, i.e. on the right of the Dapia as you approach Spetsai by boat. Overlooking the Dapia are the modern hotels Roumani and Star, while the Acropol and Saronicos hotels provide accommodation in more traditional surroundings. Dominating the Clock Tower Square is the Pharos (Lighthouse) Hotel, and east of the fish market is the Soleil Hotel. The Myrtoon Hotel is a short distance inland from the town beach. The new Spetses Hotel is on the road to the Anargyrios and Korgialenios School, and beyond it is the Kastelli, formerly the Xenia Hotel, which also provides bungalow accommodation. The Kastelli shares the facilities of its sandy beach with the school.

Name	Class	Telephone (if calling from off Spetsai, use the island code number 0298)
Posidonion	A	72-208; 72-308
Spetses	A	72-494; 72-602/3
Kastelli	A	72-311/2/3
Roumani	B	72-244; 72-344
Myrtoon	C	72-555/6
Soleil	C	72-268; 72-488
Pharos	C	72-613/4
Star	C	72-214
Acropol	D	72-219
Saronicos	D	72-646

There are a number of pensions and guest-houses, and during the high season rooms are available in private houses; for bookings apply to the Tourist Police or Takis's Tourist Office. Takis's youth hostels provide moderately priced accommodation for students.

What To Do

The clear warm water of the Aegean is ideal for swimming, diving, and spear fishing. The best beaches are on the south side of the island, at Aghioi Anargyroi and Aghia Paraskevi. There is a safe sandy beach on the mainland at nearby Kosta, where, in 1925, mixed bathing was officially tolerated for the first time in Greece. Underwater fishing is recommended off the lighthouse headland, at Kouzounos, and Zogeria. For the less energetic, fishing lines can be bought cheaply on the island. At the Old Harbour and at La Lampara tows for water skiing can be arranged and a variety of small sailing craft are available for hire.

Horses may be hired by the hour, though in summer riding is only advisable early and late in the day. During the shooting season the Greeks, who are keen hunters, shoot pheasant, partridge, quail, and woodcock, mostly fugitives from Spetsopoula. Horse cabs can be taken as far as Aghia Marina or Ligoneri, though for any ride it is wise to agree on a price beforehand. There are bicycles and motorcycles for hire at a number of shops in the town. The tour of the island is about 25 km. (15 miles) on a rough but well-graded road paved for a short way on either side of the town. Takis's Tourist Office acts as an agency for most of the recreations above, but you can also make your own arrangements. Takis organizes barbecues at local beaches throughout the summer.

In the evenings there is plenty to choose from. After an aperitif and *mezé* on the Dapia, you may either eat in the town or head for Aghia Marina where there is live bouzouki music at George's, and dancing at the Twins Discotheque. The Karnayo Discotheque is at the Old Harbour and the Delphinia Discotheque is behind the town beach. There are two performances nightly at the Marina and Titania cinemas in the town. The programmes are changed frequently and some good foreign films are shown in the summer.

Baltiza Creek: shipyard

What to Buy

Visitors wanting to buy souvenirs or presents have a wide range of local products from which to choose. Although many of the goods tend to be brought from the mainland, some shops specialize in handicraft produced on the island. The locally-designed jewellery and hand-painted articles, from dresses to wooden trays and pebble paper weights, are recommended. A wide selection of hand carved and decorated items is available at Gorgona, behind the Soleil Hotel. Shoemakers will make sandals to measure, and a leather shop behind the Saronicos Hotel has an original selection of bags, belts, and purses. The tourist shops stock handwoven floor mats and rugs and woollen shoulder bags. There are also hand-embroidered table cloths, dresses, blouses, and the traditional kerchiefs. The popular Greek fleece rugs, *flokates,* are available in the larger shops. Hand-painted pottery from the islands, wooden backgammon sets, *komboloi* (worry beads), records of Greek music, toy *evzones,* and dolls in Greek costume are available in several shops. A gift shop in the arcade near the fish market sells Bouboulina dolls, complete with telescope. Apart from such items as ouzo, olives, and olive oil on sale throughout Greece, the island specialities of *amygdaloto* and *ergolavos* almond cakes make suitable presents and they stay fresh for up to a week.

Plant Life

The island is composed of nummulitic limestone, thrust up from the sea about ten million years ago. Later in antiquity the Mediterranean basin was flooded by the sea and the Aegean area sank an estimated 3,000 metres. The thin and in places reddish alkaline soil is the result of decomposition of the limestone. The porous limestone has led to the formation of a number of caves, especially on the south side of the island and also a few springs. In many places pebbles can be seen embedded in the rock, resulting in a conglomerate which appears man-made.

The climate is typically Mediterranean, and the January and February mean temperature of 10° C rises to 26° C in July and August. The average annual rainfall is about 400 mm., most of which falls between November and April. The island's proximity to the mainland means that an occasional winter frost or snowfall cannot be ruled out.

The two thirds of the island belonging to the Anargyros Trust is pine covered, chiefly with the Aleppo Pine. On the hills, you can see the pines scarred with cuts under which tins collect the dripping resin, added to the Greek wine known as retsina. On the terraces which ladder their way up the hillsides a few cereals are grown, while olives and almonds are also cultivated. Most oranges, lemons, vines, and loquats are grown in gardens and courtyards. Other trees and shrubs on the island are figs, pistachios, myrtle, oleander, the Chaste Tree, and the evergreen Carob, cultivated for its large pods. The Melias, Eucalyptus, and Acacias which line the roads have been imported to Greece, as have the Bougainvillea, Jacaranda, and Wisteria commonly seen in Spetsiot gardens.

In clearings in the hills and in open spaces on the ridge, characteristic shrubs and plants of the maquis, Mediterranean scrubland, are to be found. Tree Heather and the Arbutus, or Strawberry Tree, with its laurel-like leaves and fruit reminiscent of strawberries, are common. An example of the adaptation of vegetation to the onslaught of goats is the Thorny Burnet, which forms a dense spring shrub, another is the bright yellow spiked Thorny Broom. The *skina* or Lentisc with its strong-smelling resin and red and black berries is a relative of the Mastic Tree, whose resin is used on Chios to flavour the Masticha liqueur. There are many other aromatic plants, including rosemary, savory, marjoram, thyme, and yellow Jerusalem Sage, though the last is not used in cooking. In spring pink and white cistuses, sun-roses, and yellow rock-roses are everywhere to be seen.

The greatest variety of plant life is evident in the spring, when the geophytes, equipped to withstand the summer drought, are in flower. Anemones with a wide colour range flower from as early as December at Zogeria. In the Arum family is the Friar's Cowl, an unusual little jack-in-the-pulpit. Tall spikes of white asphodel, in the Lily family, force their way up through stony ground in the spring. Its relative, the sea squill, sprouts dark green leaves from its enormous bulbs and flowers in late summer. Later still the smaller purple Autumnal Squills appear in droves. Cyclamen, with pink flowers and dark green patterned foliage flower from autumn till the end of the year.

The Muscari (Grape Hyacinth) family seems to survive the pillaging of its bulbs, which are eaten during Lent. Also in spring can be seen the Star of Bethlehem and the Greek Fritillary, whose unpleasant smell acts as a repellent to predators. Bright yellow crocusses flourish on wasteland behind the Old Harbour, and the black-tipped Widow Iris can be found in the vicinity of Hara and Elona. Later, purple gladioli grow on the cultivated terraces. From March to May drifts of yellow daisies fill gullies and open spaces in the town.

On rocks and walls the pale pink and white caper grows, its buds used in cooking. Of the parasitic plants to be seen, the most common are the Broomrapes, which especially attack beans, and the Cytinus, whose small red and orange knobs grow on cistus roots. Although not a native, the Bermuda Buttercup is a handsome weed in orchards and olive groves early in the year. The non-native Prickly Pear and Mesembryanthemum abound by the sea, while at Vrellou and Lazaretto there are colonies of Century Plants, also known as agaves or aloes.

Several species of the orchid family are found on the island. Violet and yellow Limodores, the large-lipped Serapias, and members of the orchis and ophrys families are to be found in spring, particularly on the walk to Aghioi Anargyroi. Many variants of the fascinating ophrys insect-orchids occur, whose flowers resemble the insects which are attracted to them purely by deception. In January, ophrys fusca and lutea are first to appear. Later come the more colourful Mirror of Venus and Woodcock Orchids (scolopax) and the Horned Ophrys (cornuta).

Biographies

Lascarina Bouboulina (1771 - 1825)

Spetsai boasts the rare distinction of having had a lady admiral in the War of Independence. Lascarina Bouboulina has become a legendary figure on the island and throughout Greece and her name is synonymous with female courage and heroism.

Her parents were Hydriots and her father, Captain Stavrianos Pinotzis, was imprisoned by the Turks in Constantinople for his part in the Orlov Uprising. His pregnant wife Skevo begged to be allowed to visit him in prison where, it is said, she gave birth, shocked by the news that Pinotzis was condemned to death. Lascarina was baptized in Constantinople in May 1771. Rather than return to Hydra with her daughter, Skevo settled on Spetsai where, in 1776, she married Dimitrios Lazarou-Orlov. By this marriage she had eight children, of whom the six sons were to be active in the War of Independence.

The memory of her seafaring father inspired Lascarina with a deep love of the sea, and she listened eagerly to sailors' tales of Pinotzis's exploits against pirates and Turks. When not looking after her numerous half-brothers and sisters she would watch the boatbuilders in the shipyard and learn about sailing and the seasonal winds from the fishermen and mariners of the harbour.

In 1788 she married a young Spetsiot captain, Dimitrios Giannouzas and, for a time, accompanied him on his merchant voyages in his ship, the Kapetanissa (lady captain), named after her. In 1798, however, Giannouzas was drowned when his boat sank after a skirmish with Algerian pirates off the Spanish coast. Four years later Lascarina married Dimitrios Bouboulis, a member of another seafaring Spetsiot family and from whom she received the name Bouboulina by which she is best known. He too, however, lost his life at sea. In May 1811 he was killed by pirates off Lampedousa, near the North African coast.

Bouboulina, widowed for the second time, inherited property and a considerable fortune, but was left with a family of nine children: three from Bouboulis's first marriage, three from her own marriage with Bouboulis, and three from her first marriage with Giannouzas. Despite this considerable responsibility, she found the time to tend to her business affairs herself and increased her wealth.

As early as 1814 reports reached the Porte in Constantinople of the size of Bouboulina's fortune and the growing strength of her fleet. Using the pretext that Bouboulis had attacked Ottoman ships, the Porte sought to confiscate her wealth. Bouboulina went to Constantinople where the Russian ambassador, Stroganov, agreed to intercede on her behalf with the sultan, claiming that Bouboulis had captained a ship flying the Russian flag and, therefore, was immune from Ottoman jurisdiction. This effort failed, however, so Bouboulina sought an audience

Kounoupitsa: Bouboulina's House

with the sultan's influential mother, Valide Hanoum, whom she so impressed by her proud bearing and eloquence that the sultana guaranteed Bouboulina's right to her inheritance. During this visit she is believed to have first established links with the Philiki Etairia, possibly through the Greek Orthodox Patriarch, Gregory V. Bouboulina returned triumphantly to Spetsai, where she continued her shipbuilding with increased vigour.

Bouboulina's flagship, the Agamemnon, was completed just before the War of Independence erupted in March 1821. It was the largest corvette in the Greek fleet and was supported by at least two brigs and other smaller vessels. It is said that, in order to prevent reports of the construction of her fleet reaching the Porte, Bouboulina bribed Ottoman investigators and had her detractors deported from the island. As soon as the fighting began she sailed to blockade Nafplion, where her fleet remained from April 1821 until the surrender of the Turkish garrison in December the following year.

An intervals, she herself landed on the Peloponnesos to follow more closely the course of events there. On several occasions she led Spetsiot reinforcements bearing supplies and ammunition for the Greek forces encircling Tripolis, the Ottoman administrative centre of the Peloponnesos, where she hastened when news of its imminent fall reached her in September 1821. The Ottoman commander, Khurshid Pasha, was away fighting Ali Pasha in Yannina, but the ladies of his harem were besieged in Tripolis. When they heard of Bouboulina's arrival outside the Ottoman camp they begged her to take pity on them, offering their jewellery for safe conduct to Khurshid Pasha. Bouboulina accepted the offer and, at the beginning of October when the town fell, ensured that the harem escaped the ensuing massacre.

Bouboulina moved to Nafplion after it fell, staying for nearly two years. Despite her sacrifices for the national cause, including the loss of her son Yannis Giannouzas, some Spetsiots resented her success and the legend she had become for Philhellenes throughout Europe. Another reason for making Nafplion her base was the marriage of her daughter Eleni to Panos Kolokotronis, the son of Theodoros Kolokotronis, the leader of the insurgents in the Peloponnesos. Late in 1824, however, she returned to Spetsai, weary of the dissension among the Greek leaders and embittered by the imprisonment in Hydra of Kolokotronis.

At the price of major concessions from the sultan recognizing Egypt's *de facto* independence from Ottoman rule and sanctioning Egyptian rule over Crete and the Peloponnesos, Mohammed Ali sent his son Ibrahim with a powerful army to quell the rebellion in Greece. When Kolokotronis was released as the only leader capable of organizing resistance in the Peloponnesos to Ibrahim, Bouboulina expressed her willingness to return to battle. It was not to be. Her son Georgios Giannouzas had eloped with Eugenie Koutsis, daughter of the wealthy Christodoulos Koutsis. Bouboulina, while not encouraging the lovers, appears to have been reluctant to stand in their way. On 22 May 1825 Koutsis and his entourage, all armed, converged on Bouboulina at her house in Kounoupitsa, believing his daughter to be there. While haranguing the mob beneath her window, Bouboulina was shot through the head by one of the girl's relatives.

Opinions differ as to the merits of this controversial figure. Stories sometimes heard about her ugliness "forcing her to seduce her lovers at gunpoint" are belied by portraits of her by the Dutch artist, Adam Friedl, and accounts of meetings with her from other Philhellenes during the early years of the war. By then over fifty, she is variously described as comely, retaining traces of her former good looks, and having the finest looking family in Greece.

Bouboulina has been accused of greed and self-interest for the bargain she struck with the harem in Tripolis. In particular M. Raybaud, a French officer, portrayed her in a most unfavourable light in his *Memoires* (Paris 1825). Raybaud, however, had quarrelled with Kolokotronis and, with Bouboulina closely identified with the Kolokotronis faction in the war, it is hardly surprising that Raybaud's hostility should have coloured his account of her. Other

Philhellenes, such as Sir James Emerson Tennent, Colonel Vautier, and Count Pecchio spoke warmly of the ardent patriotism which inspired her heroism.

Eleni Altamura (1821 - 1900)

Born in Spetsai in 1821, she spent her childhood in the family home in Kastelli, of which only the pebble mosaic of the courtyard remains. Her father, Yannis Boukouris, a captain who sailed as far as South America in his youth, actively participated in the War of Independence using much of his fortune equipping Spetsiot boats. Despite both his frequent absences during the war-torn years of Eleni's early childhood and his illiteracy, Boukouris was keenly interested in his daughter's education.

She attended the French school in Nafplion and, later, the Hill School in Athens, but her father also hired tutors in languages, music, and art for his daughter at home. Boukouris consented to her studying art in Italy, an unheard of undertaking for a single girl, on condition she dressed as a man and, in April 1848, Eleni and her father went to Rome where she entered an art academy. Her surviving canvasses of this period, such as "Despair" and "Scene from Dante's Inferno" demonstrate intense realism.

Eleni later transferred to the School of Fine Arts in Naples, becoming a pupil of Saverio Altamura, a young artist noted for his historical and religious paintings who was much impressed by the talent of his young Greek student. One evening at festivities organized by the Greek community in Naples, Eleni was so excited by hearing songs of her homeland that she scandalized both Greeks and Italians present by embracing a young Greek girl. To prevent a fray, she was obliged to throw off her disguise as a young man, which revelation so pleased Saverio Altamura that he promptly proposed to her.

The couple were married in 1852 and within a few years had three children, Yannis, Sophia, and Alexandros. To provide Eleni with a companion and to enable her to have a model without going to the studio, they engaged an attractive

English girl with whom, however, Saverio soon ran off to Paris.

In 1857 Eleni Altamura returned to Athens where she lived with her father in Plaka till his death soon after. She opened a studio and held art classes, while representing Greece at international exhibitions. Through the young Queen Olga, who was one of her pupils, she became known in the royal court of Greece. Eleni's son Yannis, who inherited her artistic talent, was given a scholarship by King George to study art in Copenhagen. After his return in 1876 he became Greece's foremost seascape artist. In painting his favourite subjects, waves, boats, sails, and harbours, he displays a skill surpassing even that of his mother. "The Sea Battle at Patras," perhaps his finest composition, combines these themes.

The Altamura House

Despite Eleni's and Yannis's artistic success, tragedy struck the family when Sophia contracted tuberculosis. They were advised to move to Spetsai but soon after doing so, in 1878, Yannis fell ill and died, and Sophia died shortly afterwards. Eleni Altamura was left alone, her son Alexandros having earlier returned to his father in Italy. Overcome by despair, she burned her paintings in the courtyard of her house at Kounoupitsa. Other works were left to rot in a mill she had used as a studio in Athens near the river Ilissos. She destroyed everything reminding her of her life as an artist, intent only on keeping alive the memory of her son's achievements.

Her reason began to be affected. It is said that she tried to recover her children's bodies from the cemetery at Aghia Anna before they were removed to Athens, and that she sat up through the night waiting for them in their rooms. She turned to spiritualism in order to call up their souls. To this day the house is said to be haunted.

But for one brief interlude in 1890 when she was persuaded to visit Athens, she lived in her house in Kounoupitsa, isolated from the outside world. Wearing a simple black dress, she would sit on a stone by the front gate, mourning her lost family. In March 1900 she died, and her body was taken to Athens to lie alongside those of her children.

Sotirios Anargyros (1849 - 1928)

Sotirios Anargyros was born on Spetsai in 1849 and went to the local school. Before he was twenty he began the travels which were to take him to Constantinople, Romania, Egypt, and later France where his uncle was the Greek consul in Marseilles. In 1878 he moved to London, dealing in sponges, later turning to cigarette manufacturing.

In 1883 he went to America, where in the space of ten years he became director of the Thompson Tobacco Manufacturing Company. Later he took over factories of his own, producing Murad and Helmar cigarettes. While visiting Greece he met his Spetsiot cousin Eugenie Anargyrou, whom he married in 1896. After three years of married life in New York the couple returned to Greece, and Spetsai, because of Eugenie's homesickness. Soon after their return he bought a steamship which he named the S. Anargyros.

He embarked on a series of projects to improve the amenities of the island, undertaken at his own expense. Having completed the fine French colonial style building behind the Dapia which he made his home in 1904, Anargyros financed the construction of an aqueduct and reservoirs above the town. These barrel-vaulted structures, in the gully above Kastelli leading to the Papamichaelopoulos farm, are still in use. In 1907 Anargyros undertook the first of his road building schemes on the island, the road to Zogeria, via Ligoneri. The following year he began work on a track past Port Arthur to Profitis Elias, leading down to Aghioi Anargyroi. Later in 1908 he built the road to the Monastery of Aghioi Pandes, and in 1914 he built the Road of the Seven Bridges, from Vrellou to Profitis Elias.

The much-travelled Anargyros was well aware of the growing attraction of tourism and appreciated how the island could benefit from the new source of income. As early as 1910 he conceived the idea of a luxury hotel for the island and in June 1914 the Posidonion (Poseidon) Hotel opened. The hotel, incorporating the 19th century house of Dimitrios Goudis, was financed by Anargyros himself and was the first of its kind on a Greek island. Apparently Anargyros was planning to reconstruct the whole Dapia area, including building a massive memorial to the heroes of the Greek War of Independence but, either because of the outbreak of World War I, local opposition, or the enormous cost, he abandoned the scheme.

In 1913 Anargyros took the first step towards buying land on the island, which had been stripped by fire, shipbuilding, and cultivation of its original pine trees, for afforestation. Between 1913 and 1923 Anargyros bought two-thirds of the island, replanting it with the Aleppo pine, which gave the island the name Pityoussa in ancient times.

In 1912 he first met the liberal politician Eleftherios

Venizelos, who was later to become one of the many guests of Anargyros at the Posidonion Hotel. These numbered politicians and the leading figures in Greek society. He not merely helped his island but made massive financial contributions to the nation for, among other things, the purchase of aeroplanes and the relief of victims of the Balkan Wars. He himself was to adopt a neutral position in the rift between Venizelos and the monarchy. In recognition of these services his country awarded him the Silver and, later, the Gold Cross of the Order of the Knights.

In 1918 Anargyros set aside money and a suitable site for the establishment of a school "run on the lines of an English Public School." The following year the Anargyros Trust, with Venizelos as president and Anargyros as vice president, was

The Anargyrios and Korgialenios School, with bust of Sotirios Anargyros

established. In the following years plans were drawn up for the construction of a boys' boarding school on a site near the shore beyond Kounoupitsa. Designed for about 250 pupils, the school finally opened on 1 October 1927. The first headmaster was Eric Sloman, a former master at Rugby and Head of the Police College in Corfu.

Anargyros died suddenly a little more than a year after the school opened. His services to the island were not fully appreciated in his lifetime, for the islanders resented being deprived of their land for the purposes of conservation. Anargyros had few friends on the island, and on several occasions disputes led to litigation. His marriage had broken down and divorce proceedings had been initiated.

The bulk of his estate was bequeathed to the Anargyrios Trust. The school was left in the hands of an executive committee, who administer it to this day. The school is now known as the Anargyrios and Korgialenios School of Spetsai, after Marinos Korgialenios, a businessman from Cephalonia, made a further bequest to the school.

The Anargyros House

Spetsiot Celebrations

January

6 January. Epiphany *(Theophania)*. Known locally as *Tis Vaftisios,* the ceremony starts with a service at the Monastery of Aghios Nikolaos, then the priests and dignitaries lead the congregation to the *Pigathi tou Stavrou,* a well on the road to the Church of the Analypsis (Ascension). After a blessing of the water, the procession moves to the Dapia, where the ceremony commemorating the baptism of Christ is performed by throwing a cross into the water. Spetsiot youths dive into the harbour to retrieve the cross, which is said to bring good fortune to whoever recovers it.

February

3 February. The Three Spetsai Martyrs *(Ton Trion Neomartyron)*. The new church, beside the Monastery of Aghios Nikolaos and overlooking the Old Harbour, is dedicated to the three young Spetsiots, Stamatis, Ioannis, and Nikolaos, captured by the Turks in 1822 while sailing near Chios. They are said to have steadfastly resisted pressure to make them apostasize, for which they were martyred.

March

25 March. Annunciation *(Evangelismos)*. March 25th is both a religious and national holiday marking the Annunciation of the Virgin Mary and Greek Independence Day. In the morning schoolchildren march to the the Bust of Bouboulina behind the Dapia, and then to the War Memorial at the Monastery of Aghios Nikolaos, where wreaths are laid. The parade proceeds to the Posidonion Hotel where a reception usually follows.

April

Easter usually falls in April. On Good Friday *(Megali Paraskevi)* services commemorating the Crucifixion are held in the parish churches of Aghios Nikolaos, Analypsis, Aghios Antonis, and Aghios Ioannis. The *Epitafios* (bier), a

71

representation of Christ in the tomb, is then carried by the congregation to the Dapia, where the solemn candlelight processions from the four churches meet for a combined service before dispersing.

The major Resurrection service is held at the Monastery of Aghios Nikolaos on the night of Easter Saturday. Often before the stroke of midnight, the peace is shattered by the sound of church bells, ships' sirens, and fireworks to mark the Resurrection. After the priest has proclaimed *Christos Anesti* (Christ is Risen), to which the congregation responds *Alithos Anesti* (He has risen indeed), rockets and flares light up the sky and people return with candles burning to their homes for the traditional *maghiritsa* lamb soup. On Easter Day lambs are roasted on spits in gardens and courtyards throughout the island.

23 April. The feast of Aghios Georgios, St. George's Day, is celebrated at the Church of Aghios Georgios at Zogeria. An occasion for a larger *panigyri* is the Friday after Easter, the feast of Zoodochos Pighis (Well of Life, i.e. the Virgin Mary), when many islanders climb up to the Monastery of Elona with donkeys laden with provisions for a day of celebration in the courtyard of the church. On the eve of Zoodochos Pighis people visit the chapel at Ligoneri, erected near a spring coming from a rock.

May, June

Special services are held on the movable feasts of Ascension Day, at the Church of the Analypsis; Whitsun, at the Church of Aghia Triada in Kastelli; and All Saints, at the Monastery of Aghioi Pandes.

July

1 July. Celebration at the Church of Aghioi Anargyroi.
17 July. Celebration at the Church of Aghia Marina.
20 July. Celebration at the Church of Profitis Elias.
26 July. Celebration at the Church of Aghia Paraskevi.

72

August

15 August. The Assumption of the Virgin Mary *(Koimisis tis Theotokou)*. A public holiday. Special service at the Church of the Panaghia in Kastelli.

September

8 September. Birth of the Virgin Mary. In the evening crowds flock to the Church of the Panaghia Armata on the lighthouse headland, where special services are held.

Either on 8 September or on the nearest weekend, the island celebrates the Battle of the Straits of Spetsai, which was fought on 8 September 1822. The town is bedecked with flags, and the climax of the celebration is the reenactment of the battle. Illuminated boats set out simultaneously from the Old Harbour and Ligoneri to confront each other in front of

The Old Harbour, below the Monastery of Aghios Nikolaos

the Posidonion Hotel. At what is supposed to be the height of the battle, a "fireship" slips out of the Dapia harbour and sails daringly into the midst of the "Turkish" fleet. The "Turkish" flagship" is set on fire and the enemy are put to rout, whereupon a fireworks display is begun on the quay, igniting festivities which continue late into the night.

October

28 October. A public holiday marking Greece's entrance into World War II on the side of the Allies. It is celebrated in a similar way to 25 March.

November

1 November. The feast of the Penniless Saints, Cosmas and Damian. Services are held at the churches of Aghioi Anargyroi.

December

6 December. The feast day of Aghios Nikolaos, the patron saint of sailors and fishermen. Special services at the Monastery of Aghios Nikolaos.

Excursions off the Island

The archaeological sites of Epidauros, Tiryns, Argos, Mycenae, and Corinth are within easy reach. For those with their own transport, the Isthmus of Corinth is a two hour drive from Kosta, on a well-graded asphalt road crossing Mount Didyma, then on the new coast road beyond Epidauros. The circular tour can be accomplished in a day, though it is advisable to allow yourself two days and spend a night in either Nafplion or Corinth.

At Epidauros, lying in a green wooded valley, is the Sanctuary of Asklepios, the healer, where Greek drama is performed during the Festival of July and August in the finest and most complete ancient amphitheatre in Greece. Usually the ancient Greek tragedies are performed, in modern Greek translations. Tiryns, a Mycenean fortress-palace famous for its so-called Cyclopean walls built of massive stone blocks and its vaulted galleries, lies betweeen Nafplion and Argos. The museum of the modern town of Argos contains finds from the surrounding plain, including the Early Helladic settlement of Lerna on the gulf to the south. Argos teems with life on Saturdays, when it is the scene of the largest market in the Argolid. A new road winds in hairpin bends up the Larissa hill rising steeply behind the town. From the medieval castle crowning the hill there is a fine view over the fertile plain and the Argolic Gulf.

The ancient city of Mycenae, the centre of the rich Late Helladic civilization and in legend Agamemnon's capital in which the tragedy of Electra was unfolded, has an austere setting for its fortress and royal tombs.

Ancient Corinth lies inland from the modern city, which has developed near the coast. The ascent to the medieval fortress of Acrocorinth, towering above the ancient town, is rewarded by impressive views across the seas on either side of the isthmus to the mountains of Attica.

In the summer Takis's Tourist Office organizes one-day tours to these sites as well as evening trips to the Epidauros Festival.

Two recently excavated sites are on the coast of the southeast Argolid opposite Spetsai. East of Porto Heli 1 km. is the site of Halieis, which extends into the bay itself. Known in Classical times as Alias and referred to by Pausanias as Halike, pottery finds and coins identify Halieis as a town of refugee Tirynthians which flourished in the 5th and 4th centuries B.C. Settlement took place sometime after 479 B.C. east of the entrance channel. From the acropolis there is a view of the Argolic Gulf, the Spetsai straits, and the sea to the northeast, towards Ermioni and Hydra. The town was destroyed in the 4th century B.C. Other remains have been found all around the coast to the south and east of Porto Heli and Kosta, notably in the Bay of Metochi, between Kosta and Aghios Emilianos, where finds of decorated pottery indicate the existence of a small military outpost of the Late Classical Period (5th-4th centuries B.C.).

Opposite the fishing and boat building village of Kilada, northwest of Kranidion, is the Franchthi Cave, a large prehistoric site containing evidence of continuous human occupation from at least ca. 25000 to ca. 3000 B.C. On the same headland in Classical times there may have been the port of Mases, a depency of Ermioni.

At Didyma are two large sink-holes, one on the slopes of the mountain and the other on the level plain closer to the road but not visible from it. In the latter steps have been hewn down through the rock leading to two chapels. The nearer chapel, dedicated to Aghios Georgios, contains Byzantine wall paintings.

Nafplion can be reached by boat, or by bus from Kosta, changing at Kranidion. It is an attractive town with narrow streets where the Venetian and Ottoman presence is still felt, notably in the Bourdzi island fort and the Palamidhi fortifications on the cliff above. The town served as capital of the new Greek state from 1828 to 1834. Its museum contains finds from Mycenae, Tiryns, and Asine, another Mycenean site near the sandy beach of Tolon.

In the summer some island steamers call at Leonidion, on the Laconian coast of 'the Peloponnesos. To visit this delightful small town you must spend the night, since the boat promptly returns to Piraeus. The town is about two kilometres up the valley from the harbour of Plaka. Its square whitewashed houses lie on both sides of a wide river bed and are dwarfed by the striking flame-coloured cliffs which dominate the town.

Between Leonidion and Monemvasia are two attractive, yet isolated fishing villages, Kiparission and Yeraka. The formidable rock of Monemvasia, which juts out into the sea from southern Laconia, at once invites comparison with the Rock of Gibraltar. In the past it was known as Malmsey and gave its name to the celebrated wine shipped from, rather than produced there. The walled Byzantine town, linked to the mainland by a narrow causeway, was occupied by the Franks, Venetians, and, finally, the Turks. Standing alone amidst the ruins of the fortress in the upper town is the finely proportioned Byzantine Church of Aghia Sophia. Below, protected by the ramparts, are narrow cobbled alleys, barrel-vaulted churches, and houses restored recently after years of decay.

The traditional rivalry between Spetsai and Hydra is unlikely to discourage visitors to Spetsai from seeing the neighbouring island. It is a busy island and has one of the most beautiful harbours in Greece, overlooked by a number of imposing early 19th century shipowners' houses which are open to the public.

Spetsopoula

A channel of about 800 metres separates Spetsai from Spetsopoula, the small island known in antiquity as Aristera now owned by the Greek shipping magnate, Stavros Niarchos. Spetsiots working there cross daily in small motor boats from Kouzounos to Spetsopoula's harbour, Aghios Nikolaos. Boats on trips round Spetsai sail near the harbour, enabling you to see at closer range the small island's modern installations.

By purchasing Spetsopoula Niarchos led the way in the

rivalry with Onassis, who later bought Skorpios. He transformed the 240 uninhabited acres into a game preserve, stocked with pheasants and partridges. For himself he built a fifteen-room villa on the north side of the island, while for his visitors he built a dozen luxurious guest chalets.

Select Bibliography

Archaeology:
For detailed accounts of Georgios A. Sotiriou's excavations on Spetsai refer to the Πρακτικὰ τῆς 'Αρχαιολογικῆς 'Εταιρίας, Athens, 1937 and 1938.

History:
Hadzinargyrou, Anargyros, A. Τὰ Σπετσιώτικα (3 volumes). Athens, 1861 and Piraeus 1925. A Spetsiot historian's account of the island's role in the War of Independence.
Orlandos, Anastasios K. Τὰ Ναυτικά. Περὶ τῆς νήσου Πέτσας ἢ Σπετσῶν. Piraeus, 1877 and Athens, 1976.
Kyriakou, Diomidis. Περὶ τῆς 'Αρχαίας ὀνομασίας τῆς νήσου Πέτσας. Athens, 1860. An essay on the island's name in antiquity.
Sotiriou, Georgios A. Λεύκωμα Σπετσῶν. Athens, 1934. An album of photographs of Spetsai in 1934, with a brief historical outline in Greek and English.
Dimitriadis, Theodoros. Τὸ Καστέλλι τῶν Σπετσῶν. Athens, 1954. A painstaking reconstruction of the pre-1800 Kastelli community.
Tsallis, Mina. Σπέτσαι. Athens, 1956.
Perilla, F. Hydra, Spetsae, Psara. Athens, 1950. Contains this French artist's own sketches and watercolours of the island around 1950.

Biographies:
Aliberti, Sotiria. Οἱ 'Ηρωΐδες τῆς 'Ελληνικῆς 'Επαναστάσεως, Athens, 1933.
Bastias, Kostis. Μπουμπουλίνα. Athens, 1946, 1974. A biographical novel.
Tarsouli, Athina. 'Ελένη 'Αλταμούρα. Athens, 1934. A somewhat romanticised version of the artist's life.
Stamatiou, Georgios. Σωτήριος 'Ανάργυρος. Athens, 1973. Πέντε Σπετσιῶτες Ποιητές. Athens, 1975.

79

Autobiographies:

Déon, Michel. *Le Balcon de Spetsai,* Paris, Gallimard, 1961. *Le Rendezvous de Patmos.* Paris, La Table Ronde, 1971. Spetsai seen through the eyes of a French writer, in chronicles containing his observations and anecdotes from local inhabitants. Both books describe life on the island before the tourist boom of the 1970's.

Van Veenendaal, Willem. *Elke dag een zondag...in Griekenland.* Amsterdam, L.J. Veen's Uitgevers-maatsch appij N.V., Amsterdam, 1966. The author, a Dutch pilot, retired to Spetsai and became an honorary citizen after the publication of this book, which introduces the reader to some of the island's more colourful characters. He is buried at the Monastery of Aghioi Pandes.

Matthews, Kenneth. *Greek Salad.* London, Peter Davies, 1935. A former English teacher at the Anargyrios and Korgialenios School ironically describes the attempt to emulate Eton on a Greek island.

Fiction:

Hodge, Jane Aiken. *Greek Wedding.* New York, Doubleday, 1970. A romance which brings its readers to Spetsai during the Greek War of Independence.

Matthews, Kenneth. *Aleko.* London, Peter Davies, 1934. A succès-de-scandale set in a Greek boys' boarding school.

Jones, James. *A Touch of Danger.* 1973 A murder mystery set on a Greek island.

Fowles, John. *The Magus.* Jonathan Cape, London, 1966. Another former English teacher at the Anargyrios and Korgialenios School set his novel against the background of a Greek island. This bestseller was later made into a film.

Other Lycabettus Press Publications

Aegina, by Anne Yannoulis

Delphi, by Alan Walker

Eastern Crete, by Effie Sapouna Sakellaraki

Mani, History and Monuments, by Dora Eliopoulou Rogan

Naxos, by John Freely

Paros, by Jeffrey Carson and James Clark

Plaka, by Jim Antoniou

St. John of Patmos and the Seven Churches of the Apocalypse, by Otto F.A. Meinardus

St. Paul in Ephesus and the Cities of Galatia and Cyprus, by Otto F.A. Meinardus

St. Paul in Greece, by Otto F.A. Meinardus

Keramos Guides:

Brauron, by Anna Alavanou

Daphni

Epidaurus, by N. Faraklas

Lefkadia, by J. Touratsoglou

Lycabettus

Minoan Crete, by J. Walter Graham

Porto Rafti, by K. Svolopoulou

Rhamnous, by A.N. Dinsmoor

Sounion, by W.B. Dinsmoor, Jr.

The Temple of Olympian Zeus and the Roman Agora, by M. Sarla, P. Evangelou, and E. tsimpidis-Pentazos

Vergina, by M. Andronicos